CatAstrology

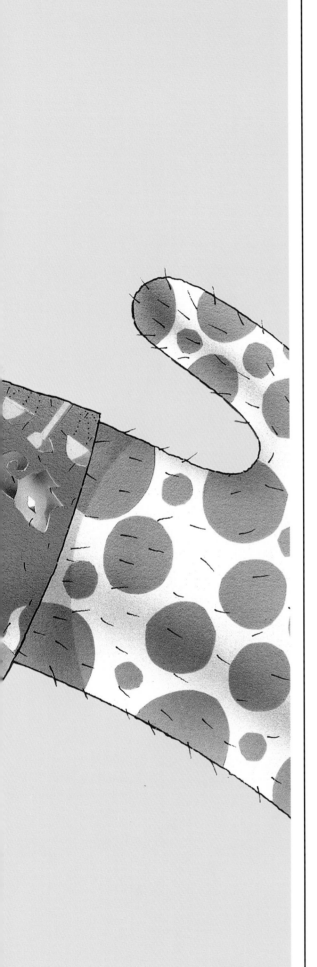

CatAstrology

*The Complete
Guide
to Feline Horoscopes*

Michael Zullo

*With Illustrations
by Ken Bowser*

A Bruce Nash and Allan Zullo Book

TRIBUNE
PUBLISHING

Orlando 1993

TRIBUNE PUBLISHING

Editorial Director
George Biggers III

Managing Editor
Dixie Kasper

Senior Editor
Kathleen M. Kiely

Production Manager
Ken Paskman

Designers
Bill Henderson
Eileen M. Schechner
Joy Dickinson

Illustrations by Ken Bowser
Text design: Joy Dickinson
Layout, electronic production: Eileen M. Schechner
Jacket photograph of Michael Zullo at the Hemingway House,
    Key West, by Mike Hentz

Printed in the United States of America.

FIRST EDITION: June 1993

ISBN 0-941263-85-1

Library of Congress Cataloging-in-Publication Data

Zullo, Michael.
    CatAstrology / by Michael Zullo. — 1st ed.
        p.   cm.
    ISBN 0-941263-85-1 : $18.99. — ISBN 0-941263-82-7 (pbk.) : $4.99
    1. Astrology and pets. 2. Cats—Psychology—Miscellanea.
    3. Cats—Miscellanea. I. Title. II. Title: Cat astrology.
    BF1728.3.Z85 1993
    133.5'86368—dc20   93-1017
                                                                    CIP

FOR INFORMATION:
Tribune Publishing
P.O. Box 1100
Orlando, Florida 32802

Dedication

*To all who have
anguished over
clawed furniture,
and taken comfort
in loving purrs.*

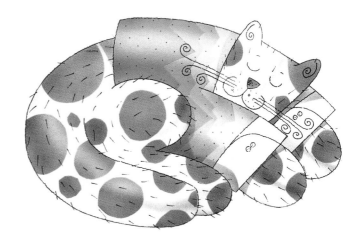

Preface

As a young boy growing up in the Midwest, I became fascinated by felines. I lived near a farm, where I spent hours observing the behavior of farm cats. Some played with me, some ignored me. Others craved my affection or saw me as a soft touch for food. I began naming them according to their personalities: Scaredy-Cat, Ham, Loner, Lovey, Imp.

It wasn't until my college days that I had a cat of my own, a mixed-breed who wandered into my life and my heart. She adopted me one cold morning in Madison, Wisconsin. Although she was a hungry stray, she had a regal air about her and demanded royal treatment, so I named her Princess.

Around the same time, I began studying astrology. As I learned more about this remarkable science, I started charting the horoscopes of friends. One day, someone asked me what sign Princess was. Since my cat hadn't come with a birth certificate, I had no idea. But I thought it was an intriguing question. After all, if the positions of the planets, moon and sun can influence human behavior, why couldn't those same astrological forces affect feline behavior?

That question launched me into a personal twenty-five-year study of cat behavior and astrology. By observing the behavior of the cats of family and friends who knew when their felines were born, I found a definite pattern: Those cats born under the same sun sign shared many of the same traits.

My professional career in the computer industry eventually led me to help develop a commercial computer program for personalized horoscopes. With the aid of this program, I was able to examine the astrological compatibility of cats and their owners. My work has taken me to Key West, Florida, where I own a New Age store, Stargazers, that features computerized astrological profiles. (Key West is paradise not only for sun worshippers but also for cat lovers. Virtually every tin-roofed house, weathered old apartment and slick new condo seems to have a cat or ten.)

In this book, I have collected my findings about cats and astrology in hopes of helping others better understand and appreciate their feline friends. Of course, we'll never fully understand our cats. That's one reason we love these mysterious furballs.

Michael Zullo

Contents

CatAstrology

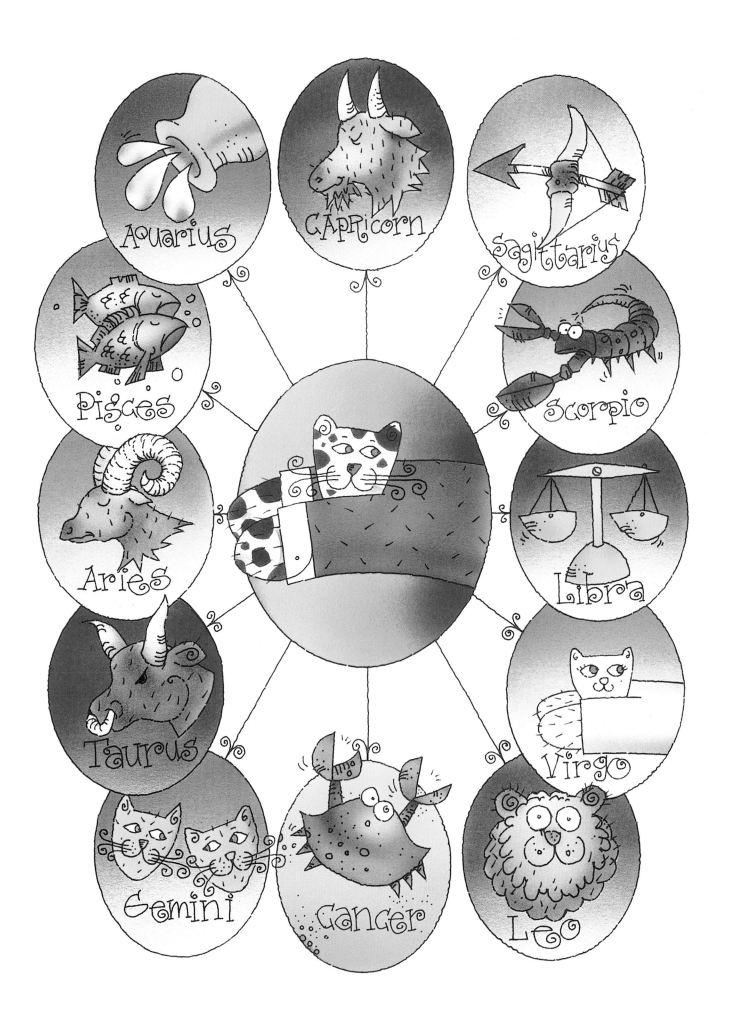

Introduction: Sign of the Cat

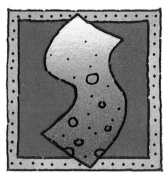omeone once said that in nine lifetimes, you'll never know as much about your cat as she knows about you. But that doesn't stop you from trying to figure out this intriguing, loving, aloof, curious, agile, mysterious, independent, wonderful animal. Well, here's a unique way to gain an insight into the world of felines: *CatAstrology*.

This book is designed to give you a celestial boost in learning more about your cat's moods, behavior, personality and compatibility with humans. It can assist you in picking the best feline companion for your pet. And if you don't already have a cat, it can help you choose the one best suited to you astrologically.

Is there really such a thing as cat astrology, you ask? — Does a cat love to climb curtains? ... Knead your lap with her paws? ... Chew on the dining-room table flower arrangement? ... Sleep on your arm until you've lost feeling in your fingers? The answer is always the same: a resounding *YES*.

Astrology is a science based on the melding of astronomy, mathematics and psychology. The positions of the planets, moon and sun at the moment of our birth influence the way we will behave as humans. But these astrological forces affect more than just people. They affect the behavior of all of God's creatures — including America's favorite pet, the cat.

This doesn't mean that if you know your cat's sign, you can read any horoscope in the newspaper and apply it to kitty. The effect of the zodiac is not the same on a cat as it is on us. Cats are not human (although some people may disagree, judging by the way they treat their pets). For starters, humans have rational thought, a conscience and a larger brain than a cat. Felines have irrational thought, no conscience and a smaller brain. (Well, sometimes they act that way — but we love 'em anyway.)

Depending on where and when a person was born, the energy fields from the alignment of the planets, moon and sun will affect the human nature of people and all the traits and behavior that set them apart from all others in the animal kingdom. These same astrological forces will affect the cat but with different results, because they influence the feline nature of the cat and all the traits and behavior that make the cat a cat.

By studying the behavior of cats whose birth dates are known, we can identify the similarities in personality and other characteristics among felines belonging to their respective signs of the zodiac. As is true with people, cats born under a certain sign aren't all alike, of course, but they're likely to share many of the same traits.

To use *CatAstrology*, you don't need to know the exact moment of birth, or plot the longitude and latitude of where the cat's life began, or pore over an ephemeris. (That's a fancy word for planetary tables.) In fact, you don't even need to know the day your little furball was born.

Naturally, it's best if you know your feline's birthday because then you can determine her sun sign — one of the 12 major signs of the zodiac with which we're all familiar.

Astrologically, the sun is the most powerful of the celestial forces, having the strongest influence on personality and behavior. The traits described in this book are based on sun sign astrology, which is quite accurate — about 80 percent — but isn't flawless without using more detailed astrological charts.

Each chapter in *CatAstrology* examines a sun sign and its influences on the cat's behavior, sociability, playtime, idiosyncrasy, health and compatibility with adults, kids and any new pets.

If you don't have a clue when your cat was born, then read the profiles of all twelve sun signs. By comparing the cat's personality traits to each of the signs, you should be able to figure out the sign under which your cat was born.

Now comes the one question you're dying to ask: How compatible am I with my cat astrologically? If you're getting along great, chances are you two are celestially harmonious. If you aren't, that doesn't mean you should boot your cat out of the house. It simply implies that you both possess strong tendencies that appear incompatible. However, there are many other factors — from the breed of cat and her environment to your treatment and care of her — that can overcome these differences. In any case, try to understand and even appreciate the differences and make any adjustments necessary for a happier relationship.

Each chapter includes a compatibility rating of the cat's sun sign with that of humans' signs. Two paws up mean it's an excellent combination; one paw up signifies it's a combination that can work; and two paws down mean it's only a fair or poor combination astrologically. (For a quick reference, consult "A Match Made in the Heavens" at the end of the book.)

CatAstrology can be helpful if you're thinking of getting a mate or companion for your cat. You can make the transition much smoother by picking a newcomer that's astrologically compatible with you and/or your cat.

This book can also assist you if you're planning on becoming a cat owner. (The term is used loosely since we all know that cats own people.) Read the descriptions of all the signs and find the cat behavior that seems to fit your lifestyle and personality. Compare those signs to see which ones you're most compatible with. You can also find out which signs interact best with your children. Then you can choose a cat that's astrologically right for you.

Whatever the sign of the cat, this captivating creature will pad softly into your heart.

The Sun Signs

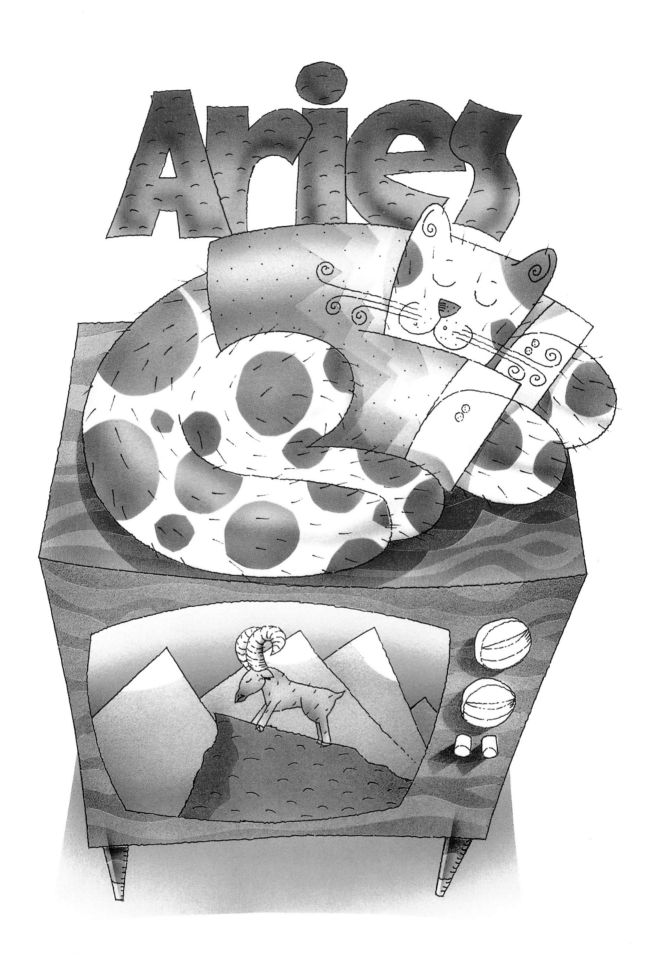

The Aries Cat
March 21–April 20

he Aries cat is ready to pounce. Full of life and boundless energy, she's a joy to watch as she plays with anything she can get her paws on — including your finest porcelain figurines. She's a top cat — which means you will often find her on top of the drapes, on top of the refrigerator or on top of the grandfather clock.

- ■ Energetic
- ■ Impatient
- ■ Playful
- ■ Friendly
- ■ Combative

Aries will race through the house at three in the morning, chasing shadows, dust bunnies or imaginary creatures. More than any other cat in the zodiac, Aries is prone to these "night crazies" — an overflow of energy all related to her primal urges to hunt and capture prey.

But just when you're ready to grumpily get out of bed and lasso this frenetic furball, Aries will hop onto your bed, nestle by your neck and purr lovingly.

By morning, Aries is pleasantly meowing and grooming herself, waiting for her breakfast. It's a good idea to fill up her dish on time … or else. Aries is impatient and if you decide to sleep late, you're in for a rude awakening. She will systematically start knocking everything off your bedside table — your glasses, a novel and even the clock radio if she's really ticked off — until you get up and feed her. She then will be a happy feline who won't hold a grudge against you … until the next morning if you choose to sleep late again.

Aries doesn't make a good latchkey kitty because she's such a bundle of energy. If you're gone all day, then make a big production out of greeting Aries when you come home. Within minutes of walking through the door, spend some quality time with her. Chase her around the table or roughhouse with her so she can release all that pent-up energy.

Snoozing on the windowsill for hours at a time is just too boring. She'd much rather be outside where she can snoop around the bushes, preying on lizards and snakes. Aries likes to show her owner just how good a hunter she is. Don't be surprised when she saunters into the house with a dead mouse in her mouth.

Her combative nature tends to get her into trouble. She won't back down from a fight if another cat challenges her. For that matter, she won't back down from the threat of a bigger animal like a dog. The problem is, she's not necessarily the greatest of fighters.

Indoors, this combativeness could at times test your patience. She will spot a fly in the house and suddenly go into her hunting mode. With her jaws quivering and her teeth chattering, she will leap off your lap, knocking over your glass of iced tea. Then she will dash onto the coffee table and skid off it, knocking the TV remote control onto the floor. With total disregard for your crystal, she will spring up onto the top of the hutch and swat the fly out of the air.

If you try to reprimand her, she will growl at you and then lash at your ankles with a one-two combination. Then she will sprint off and sulk for a while. But before too long, she will be back snuggling next to you, purring with forgiveness.

SOCIABILITY

Aries is a party animal and likes to play with others — especially her owner.

When your friends come over for a visit, Aries will be right at the door, checking out each guest. She will promptly nudge her head under a guest's hand in hopes of getting him to pet or play with her. Aries will spend time with just about everyone — except those who aren't cat people. She won't annoy them; she will just ignore them.

PLAYTIME

Because Aries likes variety, make sure you have plenty of rubber balls, knitted mice and squeaky toys around the house for her to play with. And change them every few months because she will get tired of the same old playthings.

You could go broke keeping her in toys, so use your creativity. Let her play with the cork from a wine bottle, an empty sewing spool or even the cardboard tube from an empty roll of toilet paper.

IDIOSYNCRASY

Aries loves to use her head much like a ram, her astrological symbol. To open the unlocked bathroom door, she will butt it rather than use her paws. If she wants loving, she will nestle her head against yours when you're stretched out on the couch. She also tends to run with her head down, which sometimes causes her to smack headfirst into a leg of the kitchen table.

HEALTH

The typical Aries is a slim, trim, healthy feline. Because of her high energy level, she tends to burn off more calories than most felines. But there is a downside.

Aries is so frisky that she's prone to injuries both indoors and outdoors. As she's streaking through the house, she will wipe out on the freshly-polished kitchen floor and slam into the wall … she will jump up for the mantle and miss … or she will tumble into your bubble bath.

In the kitchen, don't leave knives and other sharp objects on the counter because she will play with them. And hide dangling electrical cords for the same reason. Be especially wary at

Aries Loves …

- Having her head vigorously rubbed between your hands

- Eating food out of the can as it's being dished up

- Wrapping her body around your ankles as you walk

- Getting spun around on the kitchen floor

holiday time. Aries will want to leap into the Christmas tree to play with the ornaments.

Outdoors, she's the type who, halfway up a tree, will lunge after a squirrel, miss and crash to the ground … tangle with a skunk and come out the smelly loser … or get stuck in the drainpipe that she was exploring.

ARIES

HUMAN COMPANIONS

Because she's such an active feline, Aries is most comfortable in a large household brimming with people. She gets along great with people of all ages.

TWO PAWS UP

Scorpio, Capricorn, Aquarius or Pisces owner

Scorpio Aries will have a field day because like most Scorpios, you love to play hard. But understand that Aries will test you at every turn, so you will have to show her who's boss — a trait you display anyway.

Capricorn Because you are a committed person, you will be diligent in providing Aries with all her needs. But this cat will learn not to push her luck, because if she crosses you, she's in for a serious scolding.

Aquarius From Aries' point of view, you're the best owner to have. Since Aries is typically a taker and Aquarius a giver, it's a perfect match. You will dote on her with all the treats, playtime and loving that she could want.

Pisces You're so prone to spoiling Aries she will quickly learn that a sweet purr and loving look will persuade you to share half your salmon dinner with her.

ONE PAW UP

Gemini, Cancer, Leo, Libra or Sagittarius owner

Gemini Aries should thrive in your home because you both like variety and lots of fun. However, she may not understand your sudden shifts in mood. The two of you could wind up in your own cat fight.

Cancer Aries could easily take advantage of you because, like a typical Cancer, you are easily hurt. You can be made to feel guilty just by being five minutes late in pouring the kibbles into Aries' dinner dish.

Leo As long as you don't get into a battle of wills with your cat, you can have a good time with Aries because you both love excitement and physical fun.

Libra You will want to dote on your feline, but you will sometimes vex Aries because you can't make up your mind about what flavor of cat food to give her.

Sagittarius This could be a fun relationship, but only if you're willing to devote the necessary time and attention. You two could have a ball playing together — assuming you fit Aries into your busy daily schedule.

TWO PAWS DOWN

Aries, Taurus or Virgo owner

Aries   You will have a tendency to feed Aries whenever it's convenient, not necessarily when the cat's stomach is growling. The miffed feline will find devilish ways to get even, such as leaving claw marks on the dining room table.

Taurus   You're not into pushy pets. Aries' antics, such as swiping at the newspaper you're reading or tripping Grandpa while rubbing against his legs, are likely to send your blood pressure soaring.

Virgo   You won't appreciate Aries' spontaneity. No nighttime romping, no begging at the dinner table, no playing in the laundry. But at least you will be prompt with dinner and keep her litter box the cleanest in town.

KIDS

Children and an Aries cat make a great combination. Both play hard and have short attention spans. In a contest of who wears who out first, put your money on Aries.

If she's free to roam, Aries will seek out children for a little affection and play. She'd love nothing better than to survey the neighborhood from a bicycle basket as your child pedals down the street, stopping along the way for people to admire this friendly feline.

FRIENDS AND MATES

Although Aries likes company, she's somewhat self-centered and tinged with jealousy. As a result, when you bring a new pet into the house, Aries will need constant reassurance from you that she's loved.

She may hiss at the new kitty or puppy at first, but in her own time — a few days at most — she will be romping with her young playmate.

If possible, match up Aries with another energetic, friendly feline such as a Leo or Sagittarius, who exhibit vitality and impulsiveness. If you bring in a more docile cat such as a Taurus, Capricorn or Pisces, Aries may ride roughshod over her.

ARIES ATTACK

*P*resident Woodrow Wilson's white cat, Puffins, acted like a typical Aries.

In the back yard of the house where the Wilsons lived before they moved into the White House, Puffins would attack and kill a few birds every day. She was having a grand time, racing around the yard, harassing the birds and slaying the weaker ones.

But then, in a scene reminiscent of Hitchcock's The Birds, *the feathered creatures sought their revenge. One day, they formed squadrons and attacked Puffins from every tree in the yard. Crouched in the middle of the lawn with ears back and eyes ablaze, Puffins was pecked by dozens of dive-bombing birds until she made a mad dash for safety. She refused to step foot outside for several days.*

It's said that Puffins never killed another bird.

The Taurus Cat
April 21-May 21

Although the sign of Taurus is the fierce bull, Taurean cats are rather calm — unless provoked.

Taurus craves routine almost as much as a freshly-opened can of tuna. He wants to eat at the same time every day ... take naps at the same time every day ... and play at the same time every day. For him, security is the number one issue, so it's best to have a household that's run on routine.

If you want a happy cat, Taurus' normal day must begin with a set eating time. Don't be late — and don't make the mistake of running out of his regular food. Substituting dry food for his usual can of savory moist canned fish will get at best a turned-up nose, or at worst a dumped-over water dish. And while you're sopping up the mess, your feline will be sitting in the window totally ignoring you, hoping you have learned not to deviate from the routine.

There will be a time every day when he wants to be the recipient of some special treatment from you. For instance, after breakfast, he will meow until you get on your knees and give him a good, five-minute massage or pat-down. Or when you come home at night, he will demand that you hold him like a baby and scratch his tummy. Or before bedtime, he will expect a special treat. (This is a cat who loves to eat.)

Taurus doesn't need constant attention, so he makes a good pet for the owner who's gone all day. If you really want to make him feel comfy when you're not home, turn on the radio and leave it on a station that plays soft, gentle music such as light jazz or New Age. When you come home at the end of the

- ■ Routine-minded
- ■ Home-loving
- ■ Stubborn
- ■ Predictable
- ■ Calm

TAURUS

day, he will be purring like a fine-tuned engine, especially after you give him a few hugs and some warm, reassuring words.

One of the best things you can buy a Taurus is a scratching post that doubles as a kitty condo. That way, he can climb in and out of the holes and hide whenever the mood strikes him. Remember, this cat craves security and shelter — and a kitty condo provides that coziness.

If he's an outdoor cat, he probably won't go far. He's not the type to wander off. Over time, he may venture over to the neighbor's yard and sniff the roses and honeysuckle. But most of the time, he'd rather survey the world from the crook of the old elm tree in your back yard.

As with most humans born under this sign, Taurus possesses a strong stubborn streak. If he likes sleeping atop the VCR or TV set, then that's where he's going to be day after day, despite your protests.

He also hates unexpected changes, and he will resist — with the ferocity of a Bengal tiger — going for a ride in the car or taking a bath. In a last-ditch effort to avoid wearing a harness and leash for the first time, he will spread out on all fours, sink his claws into your antique Persian rug, and dare you to pull him across the room. Don't despair and don't yell. If you're patient and display a loving approach, you can eventually win Taurus over. Remember, if you push him too fast or too hard, he will think nothing of scratching up your arm.

SOCIABILITY

Taurus isn't a shy cat, but he doesn't necessarily want to be the center of attention either. If you entertain a lot, he will be a delight to have around — as long as he's not forced to perform in front of a crowd. Just let him mingle with your guests at his own calm pace. He will instinctively sense which humans would love to pet him and which humans would like to see him buried in his litter box.

PLAYTIME

Taurus enjoys playing with his same favorite toys. Most every day, he will drag out an old, dirty rubber mouse and toss it around. Once he tires of that, he will most likely play with a squeaky toy.

Don't be quick to change toys just because they look a little bit claw-worn. Taurus may not readily accept new playthings. It's best to place a new toy with his old ones and let him slowly get used to it. Taurus will eventually take an interest in the crocheted goony-bird that Grandma Melba made just for him.

Taurus would like you to play hide-and-seek with him or catch and fetch: You throw the ball, he runs after it and knocks it around for a while and then you go fetch it.

IDIOSYNCRASY

Taurus has a tendency to put inedible things in his mouth. He will munch on phone cords, shoes, your favorite wool sweater or even a corner of your blanket.

Keep pins, needles and beads secure in the sewing basket and keep the desk clean of any paper clips and small erasers. Otherwise, you may find yourself performing the Heimlich maneuver on your cat.

HEALTH

Taurus is generally a healthy feline. However, he does have a tendency to gain a little more weight than he should. He will eat as much food as you put in front of him.

Because he's prone to a weight problem, he risks a greater incidence of liver disease, diabetes, pancreatitis and arthritis. But if you watch

Taurus Loves ...

- Listening to the chimes of a grandfather clock

- Napping on the same couch cushion every day

- Watching goldfish swim in an aquarium

- Munching on cookie dough

his diet, he should do fine. Save those treats for special occasions.

Taurus definitely needs to exercise. So get involved with him in some physical activity, and try to do it at the same time every day. You know how he loves routine.

TAURUS

HUMAN COMPANIONS

Home is safe and secure for Taurus and he will get along with everyone as long as they don't disrupt his personal schedule. He's not as affectionate as some other cats of the zodiac, but he's extremely loyal to his human family.

TWO PAWS UP

Cancer, Virgo or Capricorn owner

Cancer   Loving and loyal, you will feel incredibly guilty if you don't get home in time to feed and play with Taurus. You will go out of the way to cook your feline friend some chicken livers. But you must watch his weight!

Virgo   As a giving person, you take responsibility for feeding and caring for your cat seriously. You, like Taurus, are most comfortable in a routine and love the security of the home. You two should get along fabulously.

Capricorn   You're responsible, dutiful, loyal and loving — all traits that Taurus needs to be a happy cat.

While you're not quite as locked into a routine as Taurus would like, the two of you will easily work things out.

ONE PAW UP

Taurus, Libra or Pisces owner

Taurus   While you will provide your cat with affection, you will both eat too much and exercise too little. Since you're both stubborn, you may get into several standoffs — like trying to keep him off the sofa.

Libra   Taurus can keep you content because he will bring an air of stability and love into the household. You will buy him special treats. The question is, can you give him the security and schedule he needs?

Pisces   While you have a tendency to overlook the day-to-day details of cat care, like emptying the litter box or making sure the water dish is full, you are a very loving person who will give Taurus plenty of affection.

TWO PAWS DOWN

Aries, Gemini, Leo, Scorpio, Sagittarius or Aquarius owner

Aries   Taurus likes to take things slow and easy. You like to take things fast and difficult. There's so much going on in your life that the needs of Taurus might be far down on your list of priorities.

Gemini   While Taurus embraces stability, you abhor it. Taurus will be lucky if he gets fed and groomed regularly, never mind that it will be at a different time each day. A warning to Taurus cats: Gemini is not your cup of kibbles.

Leo   Because of your domineering, energetic nature, you might unwittingly scare the whiskers right off Taurus. You might also feel a little too resentful of his need for a routine-oriented life.

Scorpio   Taurus will never know where he stands with you. Because of your mercurial nature, you will squeeze and hug him one minute and totally ignore him the next.

Sagittarius   Because you tend to be such an active, free-spirited person, Taurus will probably not feel very comfortable with you as an owner. You're better off with a livelier cat.

Aquarius   You're too busy to be bogged down by a routine. Besides, you prefer to be saving the world, not sitting home with Taurus. You need a much more independent feline.

KIDS

Taurus will get along fine with children, although it may take a little time for him to get to know them.

Taurus certainly will enjoy the attention from young people. But understand that he doesn't like to roughhouse. He's also the type who won't play on a moment's notice.

Playtime will happen when he's in the mood — which will be the same time most every day.

FRIENDS AND MATES

Being the homebody that he is, Taurus can be a little possessive of his things. It's an understatement to say he won't take to new animal friends quickly. His hair will stand on end when he sees some strange creature intruding into his life, playing with his favorite toys or, heaven help the animal, chowing down on Taurus' food.

Your best bet is to be patient. It could take weeks — even months — before Taurus is comfortable with another animal. But once Taurus makes the adjustment, he will be a loving pal for your new pet.

THE WORLD'S MOST FAMOUS FAT CAT

Tiddles — a stray who became famous the world over because of his girth — acted just like a Taurus. At his heaviest, he weighed more than 32 pounds!

In 1970, Tiddles was a frightened kitten who wandered into the ladies' bathroom at Paddington Station in London. He was adopted by an attendant, who shared her cheese sandwich with him. Every day, like clockwork, Tiddles would show up for a handout.

Soon word spread about the friendly cat and people dropped off such goodies as chicken livers, lambs' tongues and kidneys for Tiddles to eat. There were so many admirers delivering food that he had his own personal refrigerator in which to store it all!

Tiddles kept gaining weight and all attempts by vets to keep him on a strict diet failed. As his girth increased, so did his fame. Fan mail arrived from all over the world, including the United States, Europe, Africa and Australia.

Tiddles died in 1982, a year after being crowned London Fat Cat Champion, tipping the scales at over 30 pounds.

The Gemini Cat
May 22-June 21

emini — the twins of the zodiac — can be one of the most challenging and rewarding cats anyone could hope to own. In fact, he's like owning two feisty furballs because he has double the energy of most other cats. Never sitting still except to sleep, this cat loves a good chase around the house — inside or out.

- ■ Spirited
- ■ Mischievous
- ■ Fun-loving
- ■ Attention-getting
- ■ Clever

The most mischievous of the felines, Gemini will try to get his paws on anything that isn't tied down, nailed down or glued down. You're likely to find him batting around your watch or a favorite Cross pen that he snitched off your desk. Whatever else you're missing, look under the bed or sofa. Chances are he was playing with it and left it there.

This feline Merlin loves to pull tricks on his owner. He will make strange mewing sounds from other parts of the house. Then, when you go into the room where you heard him mewing, he will be somewhere else, mewing. When you go into that room, he's off in another place in the house — and you will never see him darting from room to room. Gemini is either one of the world's sneakiest cats or a great ventriloquist.

He's a little devil. He will sit patiently atop the refrigerator watching you prepare dinner. Just don't turn your back on him, or a piece of your diced chicken will be missing — and so will Gemini.

The first up in the morning, Gemini will awaken you at the crack of dawn with a paw or a lick on your nose. As you open your bleary eyes, he will be bouncing around the room, ready to play before breakfast. You may not find the belt to your robe — he probably hid it under your bed — but you're likely to step on the catnip toy that he brought in to play with.

GEMINI

Gemini is a streaker. If that back door swings open, he's gone in a flash. That's because of all the cats in the zodiac, Gemini is a true lover of the outdoors. He has to have his space — and lots of it. It's in his blood to explore new territory and roam. But he will always return home.

If your Gemini is an indoor cat, make sure he has access to a window for sunshine and fresh air. Keep your curtains open, blinds up, and crack open the window so he can sniff the breeze. If possible, take him out on the balcony of your apartment every day or train him to walk with a harness and leash so you can take him for walks in the park. This highly active cat needs the outdoor stimulation to keep him physically and mentally fit.

As is true for any pet cat, don't take Gemini for granted. He seeks attention and affection every day. Otherwise, he will become bored, depressed and show definite personality changes — none for the better. In such cases, he's likely to take his frustrations out on your Lladro collection. So make sure you give him some loving every day and a special toy or treat every once in a while to show him how much you appreciate him. But don't expect him to show you affection when you want it. That's not in his makeup. He will return your love when the mood strikes him.

SOCIABILITY

Gemini is not afraid of the lime-light. He's a natural-born ham who can perform anywhere at any time. He will be a hit with your guests — assuming they get a kick out of Gemini playing with their shoelaces or jumping into their laps and demanding to be stroked.

While you and your guests are engaged in a serious discussion, Gemini is likely to trot into the living room and drop a favorite toy at the feet of one of your guests, expecting to play.

PLAYTIME

Gemini loves toys, toys and more toys, especially squeaky ones and balls with bells in them. They will provide hours of fun for him. But to keep from spoiling him rotten with a warehouse full of play-things, try rotating his toys. Take a few out of circulation for a while and then reintroduce them a month later.

Because Gemini has a lot of nervous energy and likes to keep on the move, make sure the toys aren't static, like hand-sewn

stuffed mice made by Aunt Kathryn. Gemini's toys must make noise or skittle along the floor. Watch how zany he gets when you let him play with a Ping-Pong ball or a balloon.

IDIOSYNCRASY

Gemini will have some sort of compulsive behavior that will drive you nuts. Whatever it is, no amount of scolding will break him of it. For example, he might like to rip the linings from under all the upholstered furniture, dig up all your potted plants (or — worse yet — the neighbor's), or wail every time you close the door to the bathroom.

HEALTH

Although Gemini is a gregarious cat, he's prone to nervous disorders and also depression, due mainly to confinement and lack of stimulation. Gemini needs plenty of fresh air and physical activity to remain

Gemini Loves …

- Playing with cold spaghetti
- Running through tall grass
- Tearing up wrapping paper
- Licking dried milk off a baby's chin

happy. If possible, let him loose to chass dragonflies and fluttering leaves, or at least walk him a few times a week.

Outdoor Geminis tend to stay in pretty good shape. If they get injured, it's usually to their shoulders or legs. You should check your Gemini on a regular basis for bruises, cuts or muscle pulls.

GEMINI

HUMAN COMPANIONS

Gemini is a family cat. He loves people and action — the more the merrier. No house can be too loud, too frenetic or too raucous for him — as long as he's included in the fun.

TWO PAWS UP

Aries, Leo, Libra or Aquarius owner

Aries   Your independence and assertiveness will be invigorating to Gemini, who sometimes will think he's met his match. Because you and Gemini have an abundance of energy, you two should get along fine.

Leo   Gemini can handle the fact that you're not one for routine and are likely to feed him whenever it's convenient for you. Like your cat, you have a high energy level and enjoy roughhousing with him.

Libra   Although you're an affectionate person, you won't suffocate Gemini with too much loving. You relish people, parties and offbeat fun — and so does your cat, who will definitely make his presence felt.

Aquarius   Always proud of your cat, you will show off his smarts by having him happily perform all the tricks you taught him. This is a fun relationship that will keep owner and cat content for a long time.

ONE PAW UP

Gemini, Sagittarius or Capricorn owner

Gemini   Depending on the day of the week and position of the moon and the stars, this relationship can be quite fun or quite frustrating. You two will test and torment each other, but you'll also adore and entertain each other.

Sagittarius   Both you and your cat are fun-loving and have a zest for freedom. If Gemini roams and doesn't come home for dinner, you just figure he's having a good time somewhere else.

Capricorn   You tend to be a workaholic who may leave at daybreak and not arrive home until midnight. That doesn't give you many hours to play with Gemini, but you will give him as much quality time as you can.

TWO PAWS DOWN

Taurus, Cancer, Virgo, Scorpio or Pisces owner

Taurus   Chances are you won't ever let Gemini leave the house. Instead, you will want him on your lap as you watch TV or read. Meanwhile, he's yearning to dart out the door and get some physical exercise.

Cancer Because you're a worrywart, you will never be happy with a cat who likes to roam. If Gemini doesn't come home for dinner or stays out all night, you will be calling the neighbors and even the police to help you find him.

Virgo Of all the signs in the zodiac, you're the worst for a Gemini cat. You live by routine and will bore Gemini to death by giving him the same food and making him play with the same toy his entire life.

Scorpio Your cat is likely to cause you plenty of aggravation with his streaking and mischievousness. Gemini just won't understand why you get angry over his antics or why you feel a need for strict discipline.

Pisces Highly emotional and sentimental, you probably won't appreciate Gemini's independence. If he doesn't feel like jumping into your lap at your asking, you will feel hurt because you take things personally.

KIDS

Gemini gets along great with children, especially those of pre-school age. Both are full of energy and have short attention spans.

You don't ever have to worry about this cat and the kids being bored with each other. If a toddler yanks on Gemini's tail, the cat will let out a yowl, jump away and then come back for more play. He loves to hide from the little ones and then playfully pounce on them as they walk by. They will squeal in delight as he darts off to a new hiding place.

FRIENDS AND MATES

Gemini can get along with most pets, especially another cat or dog who was born to run. Gemini loves nothing better than a pal he can chase. To him, animal companions are living playthings.

The best feline matchup for Gemini is another Gemini.

The two should hit it off right from the start and enjoy exploring the outside world together. When it's time to sleep, they will curl up near each other.

Most any cat from the zodiac will make a fine companion except a Taurus, who simply will not appreciate nor tolerate all the crazy antics of the fun-loving Gemini.

THE PRESIDENTIAL STREAKER

President Calvin Coolidge's pet cat, Tiger, hated to be cooped up at home. So one day in 1923, in typical Gemini fashion, Tiger dashed out of the White House and bounded down Pennsylvania Avenue. When the cat didn't return home later that evening, the President did what most of his fellow Cancers would do — he enlisted everyone's help in finding his lost feline.

Coolidge turned to the new medium of radio and broadcast a description of the missing cat over the airwaves. It worked. Tiger was found and returned to the White House, much to the relief of the President.

However, Tiger's wanderlust was greater than Coolidge's affection for him and, a few weeks later, the cat ran away for the second time and was never seen by the First Family again.

The Cancer Cat
June 22-July 23

ancer is the quintessential lap cat who likes to be hugged, held and stroked. You can't give this cat too much loving. This perpetual purring machine will show her devotion and loyalty to you from morning till night.

- ■ Affectionate
- ■ Devoted
- ■ Moody
- ■ Sensitive
- ■ Nurturing

She will follow you everywhere. As you take your morning shower, Cancer will sit in the bathroom with you. In fact, since most feline Cancers tend to copy what they see, your cat may well wash herself on the bathroom rug while you shower.

Later, as you walk into the kitchen with Cancer at your heels, her purring will grow louder in happy anticipation of breakfast. After she chows down, you may find it hard to read the morning paper because Cancer will keep jumping into your lap or trying to get your attention by swatting at the sports section.

When you're ready to leave for work, she will be by the front door, hoping to get a few tender strokes from you before you head out. Then she will spend the rest of the day contentedly sprawled out on the windowsill, soaking up the rays of the sun. Next to loving, napping is her favorite pastime.

Cancer will know when you're only minutes away from arriving home in the evening and she will be waiting by the front door for your return. She will greet you with lots of meowing and leg rubbing. This is a good time for you to utter some baby talk because Cancer thrives on that warm, cooing sound.

If she's an outdoor cat, she will stick close to home. She enjoys the comfort of indoors much more than harassing birds in the back yard.

As you're preparing dinner, your only problem with the cat will be keeping her out from under your feet — not because she's hungry, but because she wants to be with you. It may not be easy, but you should teach her to stay out of the kitchen so you don't trip over her.

Later, while you're watching TV or reading, expect Cancer to be in your lap, begging to be stroked. By the time you're ready for bed, she will already be there snuggling up by your pillow.

Although she's generally calm and relaxed, Cancer can get a little moody. There might be times when, for reasons known only to her, she doesn't feel like purring or hopping into your lap when you want her. But these moments are not too common.

She doesn't like loud voices, especially when they are directed at her. Yelling at this sensitive, emotional cat will get you nowhere. All it will do is drive her away from you. She's likely to scurry off into her secret hiding place behind the dryer.

Cancer forgets nothing — ever. Especially the shot she got at the vet. She will know that getting into the car means a trip to that sweet-talking, white-coated person who sticks needles in cats. Cancer will turn into a wildcat in your car unless you transport her in a travel carrier.

SOCIABILITY

When company arrives, Cancer is not likely to be at the door greeting your guests the way she does when you come home. She's not especially fond of strangers and most likely will disappear until your guests have left.

You might be able to coax her out with some gentle prodding — but only for a few moments. All she needs is to sense that one guest is not a cat person and Cancer will high-tail it out of the room. Whatever you do, don't force the issue or Cancer may have an embarrassing accident at the feet of one of your guests.

PLAYTIME

Cancer doesn't need a lot of toys to be happy. All she wants are a couple of soft, cuddly playthings that she can toss around and curl up with.

She prefers the simple things such as a ball of yarn or string or even a crumpled-up newspaper. A catnip toy may show the silly side of her personality, but don't expect her to get too wild. That's not her style.

IDIOSYNCRASY

Cancer is a loony cat — literally. More than any other feline, Cancer is affected by the moon. Because she is astrologically ruled by the moon, Cancer is prone to bizarre personality changes during a full moon.

She might start the evening by pacing back and forth, whining and howling while scratching at the door to go outside. It won't do any good to scold her. That's just the way she is during the full moon. Leave her alone and she will return to her normal, sweet, affectionate self.

HEALTH

Because Cancer is such a sensitive cat, she's prone to stomach problems caused by stress or anxiety — but only if she lives in a tension-filled house. If family members shout at each other and argue a lot, some of that angst can rub off on the cat, causing her to cower under the bed. This often results in stomach ailments — including ulcers.

Cancer Loves ...
- Hearing sweet nothings from her owner
- Pawing a foggy bathroom mirror
- Listening to the sounds of silence
- Licking the tears off a child's face

Nothing will age Cancer faster than stress. She may not handle big changes in her life, such as moving to a new house. And she will have a terrible time adjusting if you're away on trips for long periods of time and she is put in a kennel.

CANCER

HUMAN COMPANIONS

Always seeking to be loved, Cancer needs constant reassurance from her owner. She can only feel secure in an environment where the atmosphere at home is relaxed and loving. She does not fit in well with a family in constant turmoil.

TWO PAWS UP

Taurus, Cancer, Scorpio, Capricorn or Pisces owner

Taurus You and your Cancer cat were made for each other because you will provide her with the emotional security she needs. You would rather help erect a kitty condo for her than go out on the town.

Cancer Because you love your home and everything in it, you have a special bonding with pets and treat them almost like humans. You will have an intense rapport with a feline like Cancer.

Scorpio You will appreciate all the love and affection Cancer gives, especially when you come home from a hard day at work. She will worm her way into your heart to the point where you might want to spoil her. But you won't.

Capricorn As a conscientious, sensible owner, you will happily provide the security and emotional stability that Cancer needs. You also like to be appreciated and Cancer will be happy to oblige.

Pisces Since you are a natural cuddler, you will spend hours grooming and showering affection on Cancer. You're the type who will stop off on the way home from work to buy Cancer a special treat. Some Pisces owners like cats better than people.

ONE PAW UP

Leo, Virgo or Libra owner

Leo If you can get over the feeling that Cancer's emotional needs could be a little too demanding for you, this could be a good match. Don't forget to give her a special treat every now and then.

Virgo You may not always understand the love this cat craves. Because you like routine, you will give Cancer the feeling of security. You're likely to make a comfy bed for her next to yours, but not in it.

Libra You can have a strong relationship with Cancer if you give her the same affection that she wants to give you. She will

be a lonely cat if you get too wrapped up in your own world.

TWO PAWS DOWN

Aries, Gemini, Sagittarius or Aquarius owners

Aries You may have trouble meeting all the emotional needs of Cancer. You don't want the commitment of providing Cancer with the affection she craves. She might not be the active feline with which you're most comfortable.

Gemini Emotionally and astrologically, this is the least compatible matchup. You just don't understand this cat at all and may resent her demands for love. And she may not appreciate your sometimes fickle nature.

Sagittarius You like cats that are independent and require minimal care, the exact opposite of a Cancer. This cat will be better off if you give her to a neighbor or relative and visit her twice a month for playtime.

Aquarius You're more likely to teach this cat tricks than give her the affection she needs. Your unpredictability may be too much for Cancer. As a result, you may end up needing to send your feline to a cat psychologist.

THE VATICAN CAT

n typical Cancer fashion, a gentle little gray-red cat named Micetto brought much comfort and joy to Pope Leo XIII.

Micetto was born in the Vatican — in the Raphael loggia — and was given the run of the Sistine Chapel on orders from the Pope, who loved the feline's devotion and affection.

The cat and Pope Leo, who was a Pisces, *made a perfect match astrologically. They went everywhere together. Micetto would sit quietly in the folds of the Pope's robes whenever His Holiness granted an audience.*

Shortly before Pope Leo died in 1903, he gave his beloved cat to Vatican ambassador Chateaubriand because he knew Micetto would be well cared for.

KIDS

Cancer likes children and the attention and petting they give her. She tends to feel more comfortable around kids who are gentle because she doesn't like to play rough. This cat is likely to let youngsters dress her up in play clothes without putting up much of a fuss.

Cancer seems to understand children better than most other cats. In fact, Cancer has an amazing capacity to communicate with babies and toddlers. This is a feline that will instinctively trot over to a preschooler and offer comfort after the child has been scolded by a parent.

FRIENDS AND MATES

After the initial shock of a new pet, Cancer will welcome into the household virtually any animal — especially one that she can curl up with at night.

Cancer will wash and help nurture most any young pet. You've seen photos of a cat mothering baby chicks. It's a good bet that the feline was a Cancer. Cats under this sign have an innate desire to befriend and care for just about any young animal that will let them.

The best matchup for Cancer is another pet with the same astrological sign. They will become close friends. However, there is a slight downside because both will vie for your attention.

Other compatible pet signs are Taurus, for his loving nature, and Pisces, for her affectionate personality. Avoid Geminis because they will do nothing but confuse Cancer with their crazy antics.

The Leo Cat
July 24-August 23

n the zodiac, Leo the Lion rules all other animals and, regardless of size, Leo the cat will think he does, too.

His throne can be a windowsill, the top of the dresser or a cushion on your sofa. You will have very little to say about it — even if he has chosen the patchwork pillow that you so lovingly stitched together.

This is a proud animal who craves the limelight. He will gain attention by either walking on the piano keys, playing with the bubbles in the dishwater, or knocking the book out of your hand. When he wants that center stage, he can't stand to be ignored.

If all else fails, he will use his cunning in a bid to get the attention he feels he deserves. When you're not looking, he's not above standing on his hind feet on the back of the couch and knocking your favorite oil painting off the wall. Then he will cower nearby as if he were an innocent bystander who barely escaped serious injury. Or Leo will go behind the potted plant and meow in a low tone as if he might be hurt. He's not, of course, but he knows you'll come running.

The more this cat is groomed and fussed over to look pretty, the happier he will be. In fact, he's so self-centered that he won't put up much of a fight when you give him a bath — because he knows getting gussied up will make him ever so regal. His majesty believes it's his right to rule the house and that it's your duty to serve him. He lives under the impression that you're his pet, not the other way around.

Leo's feeding time should not be a passing thought. Make it an event. He will expect you to call him to dinner, and the

- ■ Proud
- ■ Self-centered
- ■ Showy
- ■ Cunning
- ■ Extroverted

moment he arrives, you'd better have that food in a clean dish — no chips or cracks in it, please — and on a special place mat. And the meal had better be just to his liking or he will walk away in an indignant huff.

After dining comes the standard cleaning and self-grooming, which is usually longer for Leo than for any other cat. Then it's back to his throne for a nap.

If he's an inside cat, he has the capacity to amuse himself with traditional cat toys. But he's more likely to sit in the window, watching the birds and butterflies. He knows that given the chance, he can catch anything that moves, regardless of size. If he's an outdoor cat, he will prove what a skillful hunter he is by the number of dead little creatures he leaves by the back door. Naturally, he will expect plenty of praise for his booty.

Leo makes a good latchkey kitty, but demands that you make a production out of saying goodbye when you leave in the morning and greeting him when you arrive home at the end of the day. In the evening, he will want you to spend some quality time with him. He has waited patiently for you and he expects some attention in return for that patience.

Leo has a tendency to misbehave every now and then, usually if he feels ignored. He knows that slicing up the window screens with his claws is wrong, but no amount of yelling will dissuade him. Giving him attention — like regular brushing —will do wonders for his behavior.

Leo isn't the type who wants to sleep on your bed with you — just near you. But make sure he has a special cat bed of his own. And not just any bed. He wants something plush and soft.

SOCIABILITY

If the doorbell rings, Leo will dash through the house and be the first one at the door. His tail shoots up, his ears perk up and his eyes light up at the thought of meeting someone. He can size up a stranger in a flash and if he likes what he sees, Leo will start prancing in front of your guest, waiting to be acknowledged.

Leo craves attention. He will perform for an audience of one or one hundred. In front of guests, he will jump through hoops, do flips or stand on his hind legs. Everyone will admire you for being such a marvelous trainer and ask, "How did you get him to do that?" You don't have to tell them the truth — that Leo is so smart he hardly had to be trained.

PLAYTIME

Being a frisky cat, Leo likes action-oriented toys such as rubber balls and squeaky playthings. He also enjoys leaping from one place to another, so a cat tree would make him especially happy.

When you play with him, be careful. He tends to get a little aggressive and could unintentionally draw blood on your arms with his claws or teeth.

IDIOSYNCRASY

Contrary to most cats, Leo doesn't like the dark very much. In fact, at night he prefers to sleep next to the window where the light from a street lamp or the moon will shine in. Or he might sleep near a night light. During the day, don't expect to see him hiding in some dark corner. That's not his style. Where's there's light, there's Leo.

HEALTH

In general, Leo is healthy and robust. If there is a health problem, it usually involves the heart. He's prone to coronary viruses and infections. If he's an outdoor cat, Leo could likely be one of the relatively few felines stricken with heartworms.

Rarely do Leos have lingering illnesses. When it's time to go, they just up and die.

Leo Loves ...

- Basking in the sunshine
- Wearing a collar that sparkles
- Popping balloons with his claws
- Relaxing on a swaying porch swing

LEO

HUMAN COMPANIONS

Leo is a real cat lover's cat. He does best in a household where he's fully appreciated and treated like one of the family. He gets along great with young and old — assuming they give him the limelight every day.

TWO PAWS UP

Aries, Leo, Sagittarius or Capricorn owner

Aries Your assertive nature will keep Leo in line. Although you two may get into a few scraps from time to time, you both will have a genuine love and respect for each other and enjoy many happy times.

Leo You make a good match because you will groom him and play with him for hours. Because you appreciate the finer things in life, you will buy Leo the best of everything, including a fancy collar. You can't wait to show him off to others.

Sagittarius Because you're a creative person, you will devise intriguing games to play with Leo. You strive to have an interesting life and you will try your best to provide one for Leo, too.

Capricorn As a strong, sincere, honest owner, you will treat Leo as an object of self-worth. You will turn him into a show cat and do whatever it takes to make him a winner. Leo can rest assured that you will make his life comfortable.

ONE PAW UP

Gemini, Cancer, Virgo, Libra or Pisces owner

Gemini You have a knack for making life challenging and fun for Leo. Guard against your tendency to get bored with things too quickly. If you ignore Leo, he will cause you plenty of grief.

Cancer A great nurturer, you will overindulge Leo with too much affection, too much food and too many playthings. He will love it. But if you don't watch out, he will become your owner. (Then again, aren't all cats that way?)

Virgo As a person who pays attention to detail, you will make sure the litter box is spotless, the dinner dish is clean and there's always fresh water for your cat. But you're less likely to spend a lot of time playing with him.

Libra As a loving owner, you will make life very comfy for Leo and probably spoil him rotten. But you won't stand for any misbehaving. And at the first sign of trouble, you will be looking for another home for him.

Pisces Although you will provide Leo with love and his basic needs, you're not too strong on discipline. As a result, Leo will eventually become the ruler of the house.

TWO PAWS DOWN

Taurus, Scorpio or Aquarius owner

Taurus You're not likely to spring for the finest food, toys and bed for Leo. Being a sensual person, you will pet him and groom him on a regular basis. But because of your rigid nature, there won't be any spontaneity.

Scorpio You're not about to put up with any of Leo's tantrums, especially since you can throw your own fits big enough to scare the fur right off his back. You may be a bit too intense for Leo.

Aquarius Not one to lavish gifts on your cat, you couldn't care less about Leo's self-centered demands. You're not impressed with his show-off nature and you won't have the slightest clue as to what makes him happy.

KIDS

Because of his regal nature, Leo tends to have mixed feelings about children.

As long as he gets his way, he's happy and good-natured with kids, and a delight to play with. However, he won't put up with any nonsense from youngsters. If he is teased or embarrassed in any way, he will take a swipe or two at his aggressor and underscore it with a nasty hiss.

As long as he feels in control, Leo has the energy to play with kids until they get tired. If he's had enough, he simply takes off without warning.

FRIENDS AND MATES

While Leo loves attention and the spotlight, he is warm, charming and friendly to other animals and people.

If you add a new pet to the family, it won't make any difference to Leo if it's another cat or a dog. Leo will still want to be king of the castle, however, and may act tougher than he is, just to show the newcomer who's boss.

It's best if you don't expect Leo to share his water bowl, dinner dish, or bed with another cat. Otherwise, a new playmate will stimulate Leo and provide him with hours of fun.

Leo can get along with most pets from other signs of the zodiac. But don't bring another Leo into the house. The two will tangle with each other for the right to rule and bring you nothing but grief. The hyperactive Gemini is another cat that isn't very compatible with Leo.

A LION AMONG CATS

Morris, America's most famous cat, is a Leo.

The orange-striped, finicky, photogenic spokescat for 9-Lives cat food travels throughout the country to state fairs and cat shows in grand style, befitting his astrological sign. Morris, voted "Animal Star of the Year" by Us magazine for three years in a row, flies first class and stays in 300-dollar-a-night hotel rooms. He dines on pate and 9-Lives served in crystal dishes.

In the summer of 1992, Morris officially announced his bid to enter the presidential cat fight as a result of the public outcry for a candidate that doesn't pussyfoot around the issues. Although he failed to scratch and claw his way into the White House, Morris continues to campaign for his pet causes: Adopt-a-Cat Month and Cat Health Month.

The Virgo Cat
August 24-September 23

ou will notice something about Virgo from the moment you bring him home for the first time. He will carefully check out every inch of your home, examining every room, every closet, every corner. He's not looking for anything in particular, just surveying the territory. He's the type of cat who wants to have all the facts. Cautious as they come, he hates surprises.

- ■ Cautious
- ■ Finicky
- ■ Solitary
- ■ Aloof
- ■ Shy

If you bring anything home from the store, Virgo won't be satisfied until he's thoroughly checked it out. He will diligently sniff your new Laura Ashley outfit or the new portable TV you put in the kitchen to make sure that they aren't a threat to him.

Like Taurus, Virgo is most comfortable with a routine. However, while Taurus tends to be a house cat who likes security, Virgo enjoys the outside.

Virgo is a finicky eater and it may take a few weeks to find a food that is just to his liking. If he doesn't eat it initially, don't expect him to come back when you're not looking. He will go hungry if he has to.

He expects his dish to be clean and his eating area spotless. That shouldn't be too hard for you because this feline neatnik will not make a mess while eating. Another thing: Virgo does not overeat. He consumes only what he needs. And, believe it or not, he's into health foods. He craves cooked vegetables and other greens. Virgos have been known to enjoy munching on lettuce, green beans, asparagus — and even artichokes!

Virgo likes to eat in a calm, quiet environment. If dinner time is noisy or chaotic in your household, then feed your cat at another time, in a room far from the kitchen, or outside.

He's fastidious about cleanliness. He can spend hours washing himself and wants everything around him clean, too — especially where he eats and sleeps.

VIRGO

Because of his solitary nature, Virgo is perfectly content to stay at home alone during the day or even for a weekend — as long as he has plenty of food and water and a clean litter box.

If Virgo is an outdoor cat, he will be a methodical hunter. He's extremely patient, hiding in the bushes for as long as it takes before pouncing on his prey. He's unlikely to get embroiled in a cat fight because he's much too smart and cautious to get into a scrap.

Although he's friendly, Virgo isn't the most affectionate cat. He's more of a loner and doesn't require the attention that most other felines do. Every once in a while, he will come over and rub against your leg or beg for a few gentle strokes. When he does want to be petted, use loving strokes and soft words. Don't force the issue with him. Let him come to you when he wants a little affection and let him leave when he's had enough loving.

If he's not in the mood, no amount of pleading and cajoling will help you get him onto your lap. In his mind, you simply don't exist at that moment in time. Call his name, try to entice him, it won't matter. He will walk right by you without varying his stride. (Ah, but open a can of cat food and watch him dash to his dish!)

SOCIABILITY

If you've invited guests over, don't expect to find Virgo vying for attention. In fact, don't expect to find him in the room at all. Because he's basically a shy cat, he doesn't take to strangers easily. It will take a long time for him to warm up, even to those who visit you most often.

Parties tend to upset his routine. He has no interest in weaving his way through a forest of legs or being petted by strange hands. He will crawl under your bed and stay out of sight. He will become interested in the party only after everyone has gone home, emerging to sniff at the half-finished drinks and leftover crumbs on the coffee table.

PLAYTIME

Virgo can amuse himself for hours with the simplest of items. It's nothing for Virgo to play with a rubber band, pencil or piece of string and be quite content.

Because he has a bright mind and is intrigued by television, he would greatly enjoy watching a kitty video — the kind that shows birds, mice, bugs and fish. (Don't be surprised if, after watching the video for a while, he jumps off the couch and goes behind the TV set to see where those critters are coming from.)

IDIOSYNCRASY

Virgo likes to hide things like keys, buttons and watches. He will snatch your ring off the bathroom counter and play with it before leaving it hidden behind the hamper. He may even have a stash of items that he's pilfered. If you search hard enough, you might find your missing sock, earring and underwear piled up behind the washing machine right where he left them.

HEALTH

Virgo is susceptible to allergies and skin disorders. He's prone to insect bites which may cause serious reactions such as breathing difficulties, swelling or eye irritations.

More so than with other pet cats, you should check Virgo carefully and often for fleas, mites and parasites, especially if he spends much time outdoors.

Other than possible allergies and skin problems, Virgo is a healthy cat who seldom gets injured because he's so cautious and intelligent.

Virgo Loves ...

■ Curling up in a box too small for him

■ Cuddling with a child's doll

■ Listening to the sound of wind chimes

■ Munching on buttered veggies

VIRGO

HUMAN COMPANIONS

With his solitary nature, Virgo is most comfortable with an owner who doesn't make a big fuss over him. All the cat wants is someone who will provide him with a calm home life framed in a routine.

He makes an excellent pet for the career couple without kids, but probably not for the person who requires more feline affection than Virgo can give.

TWO PAWS UP

Taurus, Cancer, Virgo or Capricorn owner

Taurus An understanding owner, you will provide Virgo with a comfortable home, good food and calm, quiet surroundings. You are so protective and sensitive to Virgo's needs that you will quickly gain his respect and admiration.

Cancer You will go out of your way to make sure Virgo feels secure. Your top priority, though, is to keep him healthy by providing him with an excellent diet and plenty of exercise. Because you follow a routine, you will have a happy cat.

Virgo Since you're meticulous and caring, you will make an excellent owner for Virgo. You're the type who will buy every cat video ever made and keep playing them over and over for your feline friend. You want nothing in return other than the satisfaction of seeing a happy cat.

Capricorn This is a relationship in which you both need each other. Virgo will rely on you for the basic necessities of life. In exchange, you will receive the affection he usually doesn't give to other people in the zodiac.

ONE PAW UP

Aries, Scorpio, Aquarius or Pisces owner

Aries You will certainly provide Virgo with all his basic needs, but you're not very sensitive to his likes and dislikes. Problems may arise because you hate to be locked into a routine.

Scorpio This can be a fine matchup as long as you don't force yourself upon Virgo. You're also prone to outbursts, which will not work with this cat. His aloofness may annoy you no end.

Aquarius You tend to be a little lax with feeding times and cleaning out the litter box, which will irritate the heck out of Virgo. But you will get great joy out of having him around the house.

Pisces You may forget to feed Virgo on time because he's not a pushy cat. But you have a lot of love to give him. You tend to make up for any small failing as an owner by showering him with treats and extra attention.

TWO PAWS DOWN

Gemini, Leo, Libra or Sagittarius owner

Gemini Because of your unpredictable nature, Virgo will not feel real comfortable with you as an owner. You like to party and do spontaneous things — the exact opposite of what Virgo likes.

Leo You want a cat that's lively, alert and always on the go. Routine, which is what Virgo needs, is too boring and confining for you. You will easily be annoyed by his finicky nature.

Libra You tend to be more focused on your own life and may not be able to understand and appreciate Virgo's needs. His aloofness may turn into a source of irritation for you.

Sagittarius You're a free-spirited person who loves excitement and adventure, traits that don't suit Virgo. You will think he's not much fun and find him much too boring for you.

KIDS

Because Virgo is such a gentle soul, he doesn't do well around youngsters, especially if they're loud or too playful. He won't be anywhere in sight at the first shout of a child. However, if he should get squeezed a little too hard or if his tail is pulled, he won't attack. Virgo instinctively knows the youngster didn't mean to hurt him.

In fact, Virgo has an uncanny sense of the emotional needs of children. If a youngster is in bed suffering from the flu, Virgo will cuddle up by her feet in a silent gesture of comfort.

FRIENDS AND MATES

Being a little on the insecure side, Virgo may find the addition of a new household pet somewhat traumatic. This is especially true if he was the first pet.

Virgo is quite timid and will not fight to hold his territory. So it's important to introduce a new pet with a compatible sign such as another Virgo or a Cancer. By all

THE WHITE HOUSE CAT

Socks, the family pet of President Bill Clinton, is a Virgo.

The First Feline is a domestic shorthair whose black-and-white coat and white paws give him the appearance of being clad in formal wear. He was a two-month-old stray who was given to Clinton's daughter, Chelsea, in November 1990.

Chelsea, a Pisces, played with and cared for Socks while her father was governor of Arkansas. The cat spent most of his time outside (which was fine with Bill and Hillary because they're allergic to cats). He slept in a little basket in the security house next to the Clintons' home.

"Socks is a delightful cat, very gentle," said Ann McCoy, administrator of the governor's mansion. "He's not an indoor cat. He prefers it outside where he can climb trees. He's a hunter. He catches birds and squirrels."

If Socks is inside when company comes over, he wants to go outside. "He's very sweet about it," McCoy said. "He just goes."

Added Frank Greer, Clinton's media consultant, "Socks is pretty laid back. He gauges everyone when they walk in and rubs their leg only if he likes them."

means, avoid the spirited signs such as Gemini, Sagittarius or Aquarius because they will make Virgo nervous and unhappy.

Much like Cancer, Virgo is the feline Florence Nightingale. If another household pet is injured, sick or dirty, Virgo will be there to lick her wounds, comfort her or clean her.

The Libra Cat
September 24-October 23

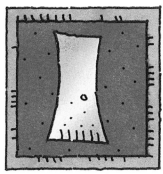

I f your household brims with active, happy people, then Libra will fit right in. She's the most social of all the cats in the zodiac — and happiest when she's treated like a full-fledged member of the family. Libra likes to be talked to and will readily respond with meows and purrs in a language that, crazy as it seems, you will eventually understand. One of your toughest tasks will be to convince Libra that she's a cat and not a human.

She will expect to sleep in the same bed as a family member, get brushed the same time you're fixing your hair and eat her meals as close to the dinner table as possible. (If she had her way, she'd eat *at* the dinner table.)

In the morning, she will sit in a chair or on the kitchen counter, "talking" away as if she were regaling you about all the things that happened during the night. Even after you fill up her dish with food, Libra won't touch it until you're ready to sit down and eat, too.

Don't expect to read the morning paper alone. Libra will hop into your lap and act as though she's scanning the headlines with you. As you get ready for work, she will be purring up a storm, begging you to scratch her back.

Libra tends to be indecisive on some things. She will go from one toy to another, unable to decide which one she really wants to play with. She's likely to jump on your lap one moment and then suddenly leap to the lap of your loved one the next. By the end of her first week with you, she will have slept on the bed of every person in the house.

- ■ Happy
- ■ Vocal
- ■ Sociable
- ■ Indecisive
- ■ Well-behaved

During the day, she will never sleep in the same place twice. She will curl up on the ottoman in the living room, then on a pile of dirty clothes in the laundry room and finally end up snuggling with the bills on top of the desk.

Libra loves to watch the family meal being prepared. Whether from the top of the kitchen counter or the refrigerator, or on a pantry shelf, she will purr contentedly while you cook. She would love to swipe a piece of the chicken you're fixing. But she's so well-behaved that she won't do anything to get into trouble. The last thing she wants is to be scolded. But that won't stop her from begging, hoping you will toss her a little morsel.

If she's an outdoor cat, don't worry about her. She will stay out of trouble. Libra is not likely to get into cat fights because she can get along with most other felines. Most everyone in the neighborhood will know her and she will know them — especially the ones she's conned into giving her treats. You can bet she will make the rounds every day to the homes of all the "soft touches."

She's so trusting of people that she will let most anyone pick her up and hold her. And if they are tentative about lifting her, she will make the decision for them by leaping into their arms.

Libra doesn't make a very good latchkey kitty because she needs to be around humans. She can cope with being alone all day, but if she starts showing signs of boredom or depression, you may want to consider a feline playmate for her.

SOCIABILITY

Libra is the perfect cat for an owner who enjoys throwing parties and get-togethers. She will attempt to get to know the guests by rubbing against their legs or spontaneously hopping into their laps.

Instinctively, she will avoid those people who are not fond of felines. Besides, she hates rejection.

Although she loves receiving affection from others, Libra doesn't like to get smothered by it. If too many people are petting her at once, she will scamper off.

PLAYTIME

More than most any other object, Libra loves big paper bags. She will dive into one without hesitation. As you put away the groceries, you're likely to grab her while reaching for the loaf of bread in the bag.

An empty shopping bag on the floor makes a great playhouse for Libra. She will scurry inside and then wait for you to tap the bag so she can paw back at you. Her favorite game is sticking her nose out of the bag, making eye contact with you and then slipping back inside. She also enjoys leaping out of the bag and impishly batting at your ankle as you walk by.

(Whatever you do, don't let Libra or any pet play with plastic bags. The animal could suffocate.)

IDIOSYNCRASY

Libras tend to make the most unusual sounds of any feline in the zodiac. She can cut loose with a shrieking, eerie whine and wail that sound like they emanated from the very bowels of hell. Libra will let out such a chilling, heart-stopping growl or ear-splitting yowl that you will swear *The Exorcist* is playing on the TV in the next room.

HEALTH

Libra has a tendency to overeat. Part of that is due to her uncanny ability to make you do something you vowed you'd never do — feed your cat a few table scraps. Try to refrain from this habit because it's not healthy for her.

Libra is most susceptible to kidney and bladder problems. Keep on the lookout for any change in her urinary habits, because one of the most common ailments affecting cats, especially Libras, is feline urological syndrome (FUS). This illness can include inflammation of the bladder, blockage of the urinary tract and uremic poisoning.

Libra Loves ...
- Playing with dangling earrings
- Making people laugh
- Finding a new place to sleep
- Chewing on a freshly baked cookie

LIBRA

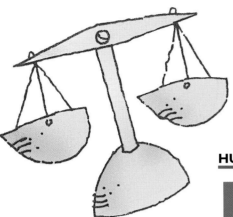

HUMAN COMPANIONS

Because Libra is such a sociable, gracious animal, she needs an owner who responds to her with plenty of attention and love. She makes an especially excellent feline companion for elderly people and the disabled.

TWO PAWS UP

Taurus, Cancer or Libra owner

Taurus   As a loving person, you will shower Libra with lots of affection without smothering her. Because you are generally an optimistic, happy person, your cat will feel very content in your home.

Cancer   Since you tend to be a gentle soul and a homebody, you will provide Libra with all the physical and emotional support she needs. She will also sense when you get into one of your occasional blue moods and she will try to cheer you up.

Libra   You and Libra will have a mutual admiration society because you're both such social creatures. You two could have a lot of fun together. But be careful about giving her too many treats.

ONE PAW UP

Aries, Leo, Scorpio, Capricorn, Aquarius or Pisces owner

Aries   Sometimes your ego may get in the way of a good relationship with your cat. Although you truly adore Libra, your temper may flare up from time to time, forcing her to high-tail it under the bed until you cool off.

Leo   Like Aries, your temper can sometimes scare the meow right out of Libra. If you aren't too domineering, Libra will be a great feline friend. However, she could use a little more loving from you.

Scorpio   Your heart can't help but melt under Libra's charm. If you're not careful, you might actually spoil her. Don't let her indecisiveness annoy you. She's just being a typical feline Libra.

Capricorn   Although you tend to want to control others, try not to get too bossy with Libra. Give her the space she needs and let her be the fun cat she was born to be.

Aquarius   This relationship can work if Libra wants it to work. You need your freedom and don't want to feel guilty if you aren't home on time. If Libra is willing to accept your moods and active lifestyle, you'll both be happy.

Pisces   You will shower Libra with love. The problem is, you don't know when to stop. Give her some breathing room or she will end up neurotic. At least she can count on getting everything she wants, and then some.

TWO PAWS DOWN

Gemini, Virgo or Sagittarius owner

Gemini   Your dual personality of hot one day and cold the next may confuse this well-behaved, even-tempered cat, who has enough trouble making decisions on her own. You could unwittingly turn her into a neurotic feline.

Virgo   You will want to show Libra how to do everything right. Your need for routine may be a bit too restrictive for this otherwise happy cat.

Sagittarius   You want more spontaneity than Libra is likely to give. She, on the other hand, may find some of your crazy antics a little too frightening. Your heart is in the right place, but Libra doesn't know that.

KIDS

Children love Libras and vice versa. Libra has the playful heart of a child and gets a charge out of darting around a roomful of youngsters while they squeal in delight.

She enjoys getting hugs and kisses from kids and will sit down all day and let herself be stroked and petted until the little ones get tired.

Libras are notorious for playing hard and then, just all of a sudden, lying down and going to sleep. As a result, Libra will only get testy if she's fatigued and the kids still pester her. Otherwise, she's a joy with children.

FRIENDS AND MATES

Open and friendly, Libra will welcome most any new pet into the household. She may be a little leery at first, and require some reassurance on your part that she's still going to get plenty of loving.

For compatibility, the best signs for the newcomer are Pisces, Cancer or Taurus. All are home-loving, sensitive cats. Another Libra is also a good choice.

TV'S MOST FAMOUS FELINE LIBRA

The leading feline on the Fancy Feast gourmet cat food commercials, S.H. III, is a Libra.

The famous chinchilla Persian got his unusual name because of the Libra tendency to want to act like a human. When he was a kitten, he and his owner, animal trainer Scott Hart, were inseparable. They ate together, played together and slept together.

Hart's friends suggested that since the kitty wanted to act like Hart, he should be named after Hart. Claiming that the trainer was big enough to be two people, they dubbed him Scott Hart I and II. So they named the little kitten S.H. III.

In addition to his commercials, the famous feline has appeared in the movie The Jerk and in such television shows as The Rockford Files, Punky Brewster and Dynasty.

The Scorpio Cat
October 24-November 22

hen you look into the eyes of Scorpio, he stares back at you with an intensity shown by no other cat. Those eyes seem to pierce right into your soul. His every action bristles with forcefulness.

Most everything that happens to Scorpio is on his own terms. He eats when he wants, plays when he wants and loves when he wants.

When you wake up in the morning, chances are Scorpio won't be around to greet you. That's because he has his own schedule. If he's an outdoor cat, he might still be out on an all-night prowl or already have started his early-morning patrol. If he's an indoor feline, he's probably in another part of the house, doing whatever he feels like — playing with a toy or sleeping.

When he's hungry, he lets you know in no uncertain terms. He will be in the kitchen, loudly demanding that you feed him — now. He will keep meowing and threading his way through your legs and harassing you until you fill up his bowl. If you're still sleeping, he's got the nerve and smarts to try to get his own food. He will open the pantry or cupboard door, leap onto the shelf, knock over the box of cat food and tear it open.

As you get ready for work, he likes to assume a Sphynx-like position on the bathroom counter or bedroom dresser and stare at you — without blinking. He's one of the few cats who will constantly make you wonder, "What's he thinking?"

Don't expect him to follow you around the house. It's not in his nature. He decides where he goes, and when.

Scorpio is very territorial and loves the outdoors. He feels he's the protector of his home and the surrounding area; you can be sure no one will venture into your yard without his approval.

- ■ Intense
- ■ Demanding
- ■ Territorial
- ■ Strong-willed
- ■ Fierce

49

SCORPIO

He has little fear of other cats or of dogs. If he doesn't stare them down first, his ferocious hiss or yowl should frighten an invader — unless, of course, it's another Scorpio. Then it could turn into one heck of a cat fight.

But Scorpio doesn't go looking for battles. He's smart enough to know that it may be in his best interest to try to bluff the intruder into leaving. If, on the other hand, the invader is a Doberman, Scorpio may take a few swift swipes with his claws and then leap up the nearest tree until it's all clear.

Whether an indoor or an outdoor cat, Scorpio will be hunting for bugs, lizards and mice. He loves to stalk, hunt and chase. And, yes, he likes to kill — but not before toying with his catch by batting it around.

At home, Scorpio enjoys relaxing on the highest place in each room: the mantle, the refrigerator, the dresser. That way, he can watch over — or is it lord over? — his human family.

He can be a pest at times, especially during the dinner hour. He will beg for table scraps either by staring at you or by making such a racket that you will give him some of your meatloaf just to shut him up.

His formative weeks as a kitten will determine if he's going to be a blessing or a curse to live with. If he finds out early that you're afraid to discipline him, he will totally control your relationship. If you stand your ground and temper your discipline with lots of love, you will be rewarded with Scorpio's unshakeable loyalty and respect.

SOCIABILITY

Scorpio is his own cat, so he tends to be a little short on the social skills. When the doorbell rings, he will be there to make sure the person entering the house is no threat. Then he's likely to disappear.

He hates crowds and parties. It's not because he fears people; it's because he doesn't trust them.

Occasionally, if the mood strikes him, he might choose to play with a family member or cat-loving guest during a gathering.

PLAYTIME

Scorpio doesn't need a lot of toys, but his favorites are animal-shaped, squeaky ones. Of course, if he had his druthers, he'd play with real mice, lizards and bugs (until he kills them).

When he plays with his toys, he flings them around with reckless abandon, grabs them and claws at them with ferocity. You will almost think he's angry at them, but he's not. It's just his way. Even when he's playing, he's intense.

He often will drop a toy at your feet. This is an honor, showing he is inviting you to play with him. Take advantage of this time because he's not the type who will spend hours snuggled up with you on the couch.

He loves to play hide-and-seek and especially enjoys a good game of chase. You can't play too roughly with Scorpio. This is a cat who would rather wrestle with a muzzled German shepherd than sit in Grandpa Clyde's lap and watch television.

IDIOSYNCRASY

No other cat in the zodiac is more vengeful than Scorpio. If he feels harmed by a perceived injustice, he will go to any length to get even. His rage is cool and calculating. Leave him alone too long without food and he will rip your drapes, knock over every vase in the house and topple your lamps. Hopefully, you will have learned your lesson — because next time, he might not be so nice.

HEALTH

Most Scorpios have powerful physiques and are among the strongest of their particular breed.

He seldom gets sick, but when he does, it's usually quite serious. However, Scorpio has such a strong will that even if the odds are against his surviving an often fatal ailment, he will surprise the vet by recovering.

Scorpio Loves ...

- Chasing grasshoppers
- Wrestling with the neighbor's cat
- Relaxing on rooftops
- Attacking the mailman's ankles

Scorpio is prone to ingesting poison. He might brush up against some fresh paint or garden chemicals and then try to lick them off his coat. Or he might lick poisons that smell or taste good, like antifreeze or furniture polish. He's not too picky about what he eats — including plants that could be hazardous to his health. He is easily attracted to other poisonous items such as moth balls, aspirin tablets or sleeping pills carelessly left in the open.

SCORPIO

HUMAN COMPANIONS

If you're looking for an independent, self-sufficient, freedom-loving cat who doesn't require much care, Scorpio is for you. He's not locked into a routine; as long as his basic needs are met and he has his own space, he will be happy.

TWO PAWS UP

Cancer, Virgo, Capricorn or Aquarius owner

Cancer   As an understanding person, you will appreciate Scorpio's strong personality, loyalty and pride. You will worry about him, but you know he's his own cat and there isn't much you can do about it.

Virgo   You will accept his aloof ways and need for freedom even though you'll never figure out why he does the things he does. Nevertheless, you will give him your unconditional love.

Capricorn   Since you tend to be a workaholic, you get along best with a low-maintenance cat like Scorpio. You don't expect much affection from him, yet when he does give it to you, you will tend to spoil him.

Aquarius   You love your freedom as much as he loves his, so you two make a good match. You will share mutual respect for each other and just enough affection to keep both of you content.

ONE PAW UP

Gemini, Libra, Scorpio or Sagittarius owner

Gemini   With you as an owner, there's never a dull moment. You and Scorpio will fight one minute and play the next. You may never be really close, but you will have plenty of memorable moments to share.

Libra   You will go out of your way to make a comfortable life for Scorpio — at first. But you may not appreciate his demanding, strong-willed nature. Nevertheless, you will still love him.

Scorpio   Since you and your cat are intense and stubborn with strong egos, you could butt heads often. But surprisingly, you understand each other well enough that you should be able to maintain a good relationship.

Sagittarius   As a free spirit, you have no problem giving Scorpio plenty of space. But beware of taking him for granted. He still needs some affection — and could use some of your playfulness to loosen him up.

TWO PAWS DOWN

Aries, Taurus, Leo or Pisces owner

Aries   This is a relationship that probably won't work too well. You have a tendency to be too bossy and Scorpio has a tendency to be too demanding. Chances are you will scream yourself hoarse trying to deal with him.

Taurus   You have the perfect personality for the owner of an affectionate, routine-minded, home-loving feline. In other words, not Scorpio. He simply isn't compatible with your way of life.

Leo   Scorpio will try to control you in terms of when to feed and groom him and when to give him some loving. This won't sit too well with you and you won't tolerate him for long.

Pisces   Because Scorpio is such a demanding cat, he can easily manipulate you if you don't watch out. Your desire to please him may turn into a full-time job of cat-caring.

KIDS

Scorpio will enjoy children most when he's a kitten. But as he grows older, he will have less tolerance for their antics. However, if kids want to chase him or get chased by him, Scorpio is only too happy to oblige. He loves to roughhouse — but youngsters should know that whatever they dish out, he will give back to them twofold.

Scorpio will not tolerate any cruel treatment. Although he might forgive, he will never forget anyone who pulls his tail or steals his toy. As a result, he will try to get even — like coughing up a hairball on the youngster's pillow.

FRIENDS AND MATES

Not very trusting of other pets, Scorpio is happiest when he's the only animal in the house. It takes him a long time to trust humans — and it may take even longer before he accepts a newcomer into the household.

The best you can hope for is that Scorpio ends up tolerating the new pet. That may happen only after Scorpio has made it clear that this is his home and the newcomer is here only because Scorpio has no choice.

Keep food dishes separate if you want any kind of peace in the house. And don't be surprised if Scorpio takes off for a couple of days — just to make you worry.

If you really want to bring another pet into your life, make sure it's one who can at least hold its own against Scorpio — preferably another Scorpio or an Aries.

The Sagittarius Cat
November 23-December 21

agittarius is the cat that won't grow up. No matter how old she is, she acts the same way she did when she was a kitten — playful, goofy, inquisitive and friendly.

Early in the morning while you're still asleep, she will hop onto your bed and tickle your face with her whiskers. And if that doesn't get you stirring, she will slip gently onto your pillow and purr loudly. If that still doesn't work, she will pick up a strand of your hair with her needle-sharp teeth and tug. If this were any other cat, she might seem annoying before your first cup of coffee; but somehow, with Sag, it's all so charming.

Rarely moody, Sagittarius is just naturally a happy feline. You can't help but feel uplifted the moment you hear her purr. She will wolf down her breakfast, not so much because she's hungry as she is eager to leave more time for fun. Sag will want you to play with her before you've even had your second cup of coffee. You will give in and spend a few minutes of fun with her.

If possible, Sagittarius should have the opportunity to spend time outside because she loves the wide-open spaces. She will explore everything from the garden next door to the garbage can across the street. She gets a charge out of rolling in the grass and climbing trees (and, yes, she can get down by herself). Sag enjoys encountering other animals, from squirrels to raccoons to dogs. Of course, this can lead to trouble, especially if the animal isn't so fond of her.

If she's an indoor cat, train her to accept a leash and then take her for walks in the park, or let her get some fresh air on your apartment balcony.

- ■ Playful
- ■ Daring
- ■ Curious
- ■ Messy
- ■ Gregarious

SAGITTARIUS

At the very least, Sag should have a kitty condo designed like a tree or a fake potted tree to climb. She loves challenge and high places. There may be times when your heart skips a beat because Sag is walking along the edge of your roof or making a seemingly impossible leap from the top of the bookshelf to the windowsill. Don't be surprised if you see her swinging from one of your hanging plants.

Sagittarius is the quintessential curious cat. Expect to find her in the oddest places: exploring behind the furnace in the basement … snooping in an open drawer of your desk … sniffing around the cleansers underneath the bathroom sink. (Always check the refrigerator and the dryer before closing them. It's just like a Sag to hop in when the door is open.)

Sag tends to be on the clumsy side, and may often unintentionally knock over the flower vase on the coffee table or scatter the pages of that important report you had lying on your desk.

She's also the messiest cat in the zodiac. She will have more food and water out of her dishes and onto the floor than in them. And if you don't sweep up around her litter box every day, you won't be able to see the floor by evening from all the litter she has kicked out.

SOCIABILITY

Sagittarius loves people. A kind word, a pat on the head, and your guest is instantly Sag's best friend.

It's not that she craves affection so much as it is she likes the attention. She gets such a kick out of people making a fuss over her that she will go from one guest to another, testing out their laps.

Sag also has a flair for the dramatic to gain a little attention. If there's a crowd in the room, she's likely to proudly trot in with a live snake in her mouth to show off her hunting skills. Needless to say, she will gain plenty of attention.

PLAYTIME

Among her favorite toys are furry ones, like a fake foxtail that she can embrace while on her back and attack furiously with her back claws. She also likes soft, stuffed, animal-shaped playthings and really goes crazy over objects like toy birds dangling from a string so she can bat at them.

Make sure she has plenty of toys. Sag is not the type who will lie on the windowsill all day, napping until you come home.

She bores easily and will make up her own games and toys — often at your expense. She will yank the drapery pull, or the wires behind your stereo, or the tassels of your crocheted cushion if she has nothing better to do.

She also likes to play with her toys in the wee hours of the morning. That thumping you hear at 3 a.m. is not a burglar, it's just Sag knocking around her favorite plaything.

IDIOSYNCRASY

Whether you live in a big house or a tiny apartment, there will be times when Sagittarius will seemingly disappear without a trace. You can search high and low, call her name, offer special treats and you still won't find her. She will discover the cleverest places to hide — curling up inside a water can on the porch, or an old tire in the garage, or a cabinet in the kitchen — and force you into a game of hide-and-seek.

Sagittarius Loves …

- Climbing fences
- Playing in a sandbox
- Stalking snakes
- Snoozing under a shade tree in the summer

HEALTH

Sagittarius is a pretty healthy cat, who's so energetic that she will exercise herself almost to the point of exhaustion.

She's prone to untimely death, either by accident, such as getting hit by a car, or by fighting, if she's ambushed by a mean dog or a tougher cat. It's not unusual for Sag to end up at the vet after some crazy mishap. She will hop into an open fishing tackle box and get herself hooked on a dozen lures. Or she will get bonked on the head by a toaster after pulling its cord off the kitchen counter.

57

HUMAN COMPANIONS

Sagittarius is a wonderful pet for an active owner or family. She thrives in a house that abounds with laughter and has that lived-in feeling. She matches up well with an owner who's informal, laid-back and not the most orderly person.

TWO PAWS UP

Gemini, Libra, Sagittarius or Aquarius owner

Gemini   With you and Sag living together, your home will be like a three-ring circus. You're both fun-loving and good-natured and will spend hours horsing around with each other.

Libra   Sag will help keep you young and put some spontaneity into your life. You will share many delightful days and nights together. More than with other owners in the zodiac, Sag will give you the affection you need.

Sagittarius   You will think Sag is a riot and couldn't care less that she's a little messy. (After all, you're no neatnik yourself.) Life is to be enjoyed, and you get great pleasure from your cat's zest for fun.

Aquarius   You will never cease to be amazed by Sag's escapades. You may try to outdo her, but chances are you will fail. You will never try to hold back this cat from doing what she wants because you understand her.

ONE PAW UP

Aries, Taurus, Leo or Scorpio owner

Aries   You and Sag are both energetic, exuberant creatures, yet at times you can be a little bossy. Ease up and let some of her playfulness rub off on you.

Taurus   You can have a good relationship with Sag as long as you realize that you can't change her. If you let her remain a young-at-heart feline, you two will be quite compatible.

Leo   At times, Sag's antics might be too much for you and you may not appreciate it when she upstages you in front of others. But overall, you two should be able to get along after some adjustments.

Scorpio   You probably won't find Sag's actions all that amusing to you at first. But she will warm up your heart and before long you will realize how much brighter your life is with her around.

TWO PAWS DOWN

Cancer, Virgo, Capricorn or Pisces owner

Cancer   This is definitely not a match made in kitty heaven. You will want to smother Sag with love and will constantly worry about her. Although your intentions are sincere, Sag will resent them.

Virgo   Because you are meticulous and demand orderliness, Sag is not for you. You will spend half your time cleaning up after her and the other half trying to keep her out of trouble.

Capricorn   You probably won't appreciate Sag's fun-loving ways. You will spend too much time trying to discipline her or train her to behave in ways that go against her nature.

Pisces   Although you may find Sag charming and her actions cute, you will have trouble understanding her. You will want to lavish her with treats and loving when she really wants you to play with her and let her romp.

KIDS

If you have children, Sagittarius is just one more. The kids will think she's one of them — and she will, too. They will get along great because of their boundless energy and short attention spans.

Sag will be in seventh heaven as long as the children want to play chase or hide-and-seek with her.

FRIENDS AND MATES

Sagittarius loves other animals and will play with virtually any other pet who's willing to play with her. She doesn't care if the newcomer is a puppy or a kitten.

Sag is willing to share most anything with her new companion. She's not possessive of her food or her litter box.

Be warned: If you bring another Sag into the house, look out! These two will be racing, leaping and brawling (for fun) at all hours of the day and night. Make sure you've secured anything breakable. (Better yet, hide those cherished heirlooms.)

You might be better off choosing a more sedate companion for Sag.

CURIOSITY NEARLY KILLED THIS CAT

Like a typical Sagittarius, Norris, a year-old gray cat, found a nifty hidey-hole — and wound up trapped for a month without food or water 1,400 miles away from home.

In 1991, Norris wandered into a factory where mobile homes are built. She meandered into a nearly-completed mobile home and found a comfy spot to sleep between the partially-completed ceiling and the roof. Later that day, workers finished installing the ceiling tiles, unwittingly trapping Norris.

Four weeks later, the mobile home had been transported from Tennessee to Old Town, Maine. Prospective buyers stepped inside the home and heard loud meows. They pulled down a ceiling tile and were stunned when Norris leaped down onto the floor.

Although he was weak and dehydrated, Norris made a full recovery — and was kept by the couple who bought the mobile home.

59

The Capricorn Cat
December 22-January 20

ost of the signs of the zodiac have strong characteristics which are easily identifiable by behavior and personality. However, Capricorn is a little tricky.

What you see may not always be what you get. She has a way of using whatever behavior is needed to get what she wants.

■ **Crafty**
■ **Persistent**
■ **Reserved**
■ **Moody**
■ **Possessive**

For example, let's say she wants her breakfast early.

You wake up half an hour earlier than usual and you don't know why. You see your cat curled up asleep on the floor. Little did you know that Capricorn subtly woke you up by pawing gently at your feet or sniffing at your ear. The minute you started to stir, she jumped off the bed and pretended to be asleep.

Hearing you up, Capricorn yawns and jumps on the bed for some loving. Then she trots triumphantly into the kitchen and waits for you to feed her. She had carefully orchestrated the early breakfast — and you didn't even realize it.

While Capricorn may appear stubborn, she really isn't.

However, she is persistent. She will patiently wait until she gets what she wants. For instance, if she's used to being outdoors and you want to keep her inside because it's raining, she will bang on the back door and meow for as long as it takes before you finally give in.

Although Capricorn is a well-behaved cat, she doesn't take no for an answer. If one way doesn't work to get what she wants, she will try another ... and another. Fortunately, she doesn't have a whole lot of demands. If you stick to your guns and don't relent, chances are she will go into one of her moods and want to be left alone for hours at a stretch. These moods may cause her to sulk, not eat or simply be antisocial. When these moments occur, just leave her alone. She will let you know when she's ready to "join the living" again.

Capricorn likes being near her human. At her best moments, she will jump into your lap and purr loudly as you scratch her chin. To get this affection, you will have to instigate it with some invitingly soft words. But she will always be there for you. She will sense immediately if you're having a bad day or aren't feeling well and need something warm and fuzzy to hold. She will stay with you for as long as you need.

Being a possessive feline, she tends to choose one or two members of the family with whom she develops a special attachment. She can get a little jealous of other people when they garner all the attention of her favorite humans.

Capricorn will spend a good deal of time cleaning and grooming herself. She likes to look good and will be meticulous in getting rid of any lint, dust or dirt off her coat. That's not to say she minds getting dirty. Outside, she will romp around in the garden swatting at butterflies or chasing birds. If she's an indoor cat, she will be content to roll around the floor with her toys.

Emotionally, Capricorn seems to grow up faster than other felines. Even as a kitten, she acts older than she really is. It's as if she's been mature since the day she was weaned. You won't find her acting goofy or impetuous.

She's cautious and reserved, but she will display enough affection and playfulness to keep her from being an old feline fuddy-duddy.

SOCIABILITY

Capricorn is not fearful of strangers, but she's not about to jump into your guests' laps the moment they say, "Oh, what a pretty cat!" She will be tentative at first and want to check them out slowly and deliberately. But before long, she will be purring contentedly at their feet.

However, don't expect her to perform any antics for your company. Rarely has any owner described his Capricorn cat as a clown or a ham. Depending solely on her mood, Capricorn may choose to let guests pet her or choose to ignore them totally.

PLAYTIME

Because Capricorn is the most possessive cat in the zodiac, she tends to hide her toys so no one will pick them up and move them. You're likely to find her playthings behind or under the couch.

Don't grab one of her toys unless you want to risk having Capricorn rake her claws across your hand. She will decide if and when it's okay for you to play with her things.

When she does play with her toys, she's not likely to do it in the middle of the room. She doesn't feel safe with them out in the open like that.

IDIOSYNCRASY

Capricorn has a habit of annoying people who hate cats.

Like a heat-seeking missile, she will target them and deliberately cause them grief. The more they try to shoo her away, the more she will harass them. She will pretend to be a loving, sweet feline and jump into their laps when, in fact, she knows it will get a rise out of them. Or she will purposely lay down in their path so they have to step around her. As they walk past her, she will pretend to be startled and attack their ankles.

Capricorn Loves …

- Snoozing by the fireplace
- Sniffing mint
- Being held by a child
- Snuggling under your covers

HEALTH

Capricorn generally enjoys a good life and often lives to a ripe old age.

However, she is prone to health problems with her teeth and gums. She's particularly susceptible to periodontal disease, in which bacteria infect the gums and can erode the bone and tissues that connect the gum to the teeth. She's also prone to gingivitis, an inflammation of the gums frequently caused by decayed teeth or pockets of plaque and tartar below the gum line.

You should examine Capricorn's mouth frequently for any signs of dental problems.

CAPRICORN

HUMAN COMPANIONS

Capricorn needs time to warm up to her owners. But once she does, she is an extremely loyal cat.

She likes a household that doesn't have much excitement or change. She makes an excellent pet for elderly people because she doesn't need much active attention to keep her content.

TWO PAWS UP

Taurus, Cancer or Virgo owner

Taurus   A perfect owner for Capricorn, you will provide her with a homey, secure feeling. Because you are a warm person, you will be very understanding and respectful of your feline. And she will respond lovingly to you.

Cancer   Although you tend to get a little moody, you will give Capricorn lots of love and reassurance. There may be a few rough spots when she gets moody, too. But your fondness for each other will make this a warm matchup.

Virgo   Loyalty is one of your stronger traits, so you will appreciate Capricorn's devotion to her human family. You will always be there for her — and she will be there for you whenever you're feeling blue.

ONE PAW UP

Leo, Libra, Capricorn, Aquarius or Pisces owner

Leo   With all the dynamics of your life, make sure you leave time for Capricorn. She needs to feel secure and enjoys getting a certain amount of affection. However, she can drive you nuts with her persistence.

Libra   This relationship can work as long as you don't let Capricorn take over the house. It's not your nature to be assertive, but you may have to be in order to keep her in line.

Capricorn   If you don't watch out, you might be a little too strict toward your feline. Because you both are so persistent, there could be friction. However, over time, you two should enjoy a delightful relationship.

Aquarius   Freedom-loving and often a bit unconventional, you may find Capricorn a little too dull for you. However, you will be loving and affectionate toward her as she will be to you — if you let her.

Pisces   Because Capricorn may not be at the front door to greet you, don't think she doesn't love you. Go ahead and give her all the affection you want. But temper it with discipline or else it will be her house, not yours.

TWO PAWS DOWN

Aries, Gemini, Scorpio or Sagittarius owner

Aries   A tad too energetic for Capricorn's tastes, you might have trouble getting her to leave the comfort of her kitty bed. She's wary of you because she's not sure what you're going to do next — and neither are you.

Gemini   This isn't a good matchup because you're fun-loving and prankish while Capricorn tends to be reserved. Besides, you like a household full of excitement. You need a livelier cat.

Scorpio   Because you tend to be very moody, Capricorn may not know where you stand. One moment you're cuddling her, the next you're ignoring her. She won't feel very emotionally secure.

Sagittarius   Although you mean well, you won't pay attention to details such as feeding times for your cat. Capricorn likes a routine, which you aren't likely to provide.

KIDS

Like most cats, Capricorn enjoys the attention and affection that children give so freely. She has an instinctive feeling for young children. She will almost never scratch or play rough with kids. She seems to understand and tolerate them — even if they dress her up in doll clothes or pull her tail. At worst, she will yowl and walk away.

Capricorn will also be quite protective of infants. She will stand guard while a baby is sleeping in the crib and she will patrol the room if an unfamiliar person is holding the baby. She might even growl if she doesn't trust the stranger.

FRIENDS AND MATES

Bringing other animals into Capricorn's life can be very rewarding for both you and your cat. Since she's acted like an adult feline from her kittenhood, she can get along fine with a companion who stays out of mischief.

If you get a new kitten, Capricorn will immediately take charge as if it were her own offspring — even to the point of overprotection. She may nip at anyone who plays a little too rough with the kitty.

It's best to introduce a newcomer who has a sign that likes being nurtured, such as a Cancer or Taurus. Try to avoid adding a Gemini or Sagittarius pet to the household because chances are good Capricorn will not get along with either of them. She will never forget who tried to eat her food, play with her toy or mess up her litter box — and she will never warm up to such a pet. In this case, the best you can hope for is that Capricorn will tolerate the newcomer.

KITTY LITTER

*P*ercy, a mixed-breed cat who had one of the world's largest litters, was thought to be a Capricorn.

On July 7, 1978, Percy, owned by Betty Gallaway of Estevan, Saskatchewan, gave birth to thirteen kittens — and all but one survived. Percy's amazing delivery nearly matched the largest recorded litter in which all the kittens survived — fourteen — delivered by a Persian cat in South Africa in 1974.

Because cats have only eight teats, Percy was faced with a dilemma over how to feed her dozen newborns without slighting any of them. Like a typical Capricorn, she came up with a clever solution. She divided her brood into two groups and placed them in opposite corners of the room. Percy nursed six kittens in one corner and, when she was finished, headed across the room and fed the other six. Through these two "seatings," Percy managed to successfully and lovingly rear her young.

The Aquarius Cat
January 21-February 19

quarius is typically a bright, friendly, easygoing cat. But just when you have him figured out, he does something so bizarre that you will wonder if he's sniffed too much dust from the litter box. He could be the Georgia cat who played with an unattended rifle and accidentally shot his owner in the back ... the Virginia tabby who ended up trapped in a vending machine for a month ... or the Florida calico who, while playing with the phone, dialed 911. (Yes, these feline fiascoes really did happen, in 1991 and 1992.)

You never know what Aquarius is going to do from one minute to the next. He will beg for food at the dinner table with such passion that you will swear he hasn't eaten in a week. Then, just as you are about to give him a piece of your chicken, he dashes off to swat at a fly buzzing around in the next room.

This is a cat of action. Aquarius probably sleeps less than any other feline in the zodiac. He really craves the outdoors because there's so much to do. There are plants to shred, garbage bags to rip open, birds' nests to raid.

There's not an open doorway this inquisitive cat won't try to walk through, whether it's the neighbors' garage door or even their open window. Every hole in the ground needs to be explored, every nook and cranny needs to be investigated, every new smell needs to be sniffed. He could be under the hood of your car, on top of your neighbor's pool slide or inside your baby grand.

Aquarius loves being around people and is smart enough to act cute just so he can get a treat from one of your friendly neighbors down the street. He will hold court on your driveway and greet everyone who walks by.

- ■ Unpredictable
- ■ Frisky
- ■ Curious
- ■ Attention-getting
- ■ Sociable

67

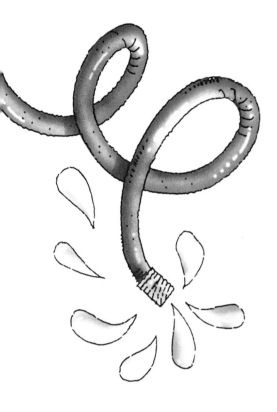

He craves attention — the more, the merrier. If there's a crowd, he wants to be there. To Aquarius, quantity is better than quality. The more people or animals, the more he enjoys it.

If you ignore Aquarius, look out. He will go out of his way to capture your attention — like pulling the tablecloth off the dining room table or climbing on the roof and refusing to come down until you go to the trouble of getting out the ladder.

This cat loves the dark. His favorite time to play is in the middle of the night. He enjoys streaking from one end of the house to the other, finishing off with a flying leap onto your bed. By the time you bolt awake wondering what's happened, he's taken off on another mad dash through, around and over the living room furniture.

While not fussy about his food or his litter box, Aquarius does seek affection. He will curl up in your lap, purring away and expecting you to stroke him. Or he will lie belly-up on the floor, making it irresistible for you to walk by without scratching his tummy.

Aquarius is not the easiest cat to train. It's not that he's dumb. It's just that he has a short attention span ... and a bad memory. When you start yelling at him to get out of the hamper, he will have forgotten that you scolded him for doing the same thing the day before. You might as well give up getting angry and enjoy him for his antics.

SOCIABILITY

When you entertain friends or relatives, Aquarius will make sure that he's part of the entertainment. Whether he claws at the argyle socks Uncle Steve is wearing or swipes the olive out of Cousin Barbara's martini and juggles it, Aquarius will make sure everyone in the room knows he's there.

Accept the fact that he will do something zany to cause your guests to enjoy him … or curse him.

PLAYTIME

Aquarius can play with just about anything and have a good time. His favorite toy will be whatever he's playing with at the moment. Usually, it's something that's not a real toy. There's nothing like playing with that leather belt you just bought … the baseball autographed by Willie Mays that you've cherished since grade school … or the wedding ring you left near the kitchen sink.

IDIOSYNCRASY

Aquarius seems to have a psychic ability to foresee danger before it happens. He's the cat who wakes up the family in the middle of the night before they smell smoke. He's the cat who yowls moments before a violent thunderstorm roars through the area.

If he's acting stranger than usual, pay attention! He might be warning you of impending danger.

HEALTH

Aquarius has a tendency to suffer from fractures, dislocations and sprains. With his helter-skelter nature, he will occasionally come home limping. He's liable to tumble out of a tree, fight a losing battle with the dog down the street or get his paw stuck in the sliding glass door.

If he ever learned to slow down, he'd be pretty healthy. But he sometimes snoops in areas where he shouldn't and could end up in a raccoon trap or down a drainpipe.

Aquarius Loves …

- Batting ice cubes around on the kitchen floor
- Dipping his paws into a sink full of water
- Playing with the telephone
- Chewing baby's breath off your flower arrangement

AQUARIUS

HUMAN COMPANIONS

Aquarius is a special feline who requires a special owner — one who will give him his freedom and let him be the impetuous, gregarious cat he was born to be. He thrives in an unconventional household where there is a lot going on.

TWO PAWS UP

Gemini, Sagittarius or Aquarius owner

Gemini   Because you love variety, Aquarius will be delighted with the constant changes in his life. Whether you bring home new friends every week, rearrange the furniture every month or move every year, Aquarius will feel like each day is a new challenge — and a fun one at that.

Sagittarius   Your enthusiasm for life will make Aquarius one happy cat. You two are on the same wavelength, providing each other with just the right amount of attention, fun and affection.

Aquarius   You will make an ideal companion for your feline. Emotionally, you are mirror images and have a great understanding of each other. His antics will have you in stitches — mostly figuratively, but sometimes literally.

ONE PAW UP

Aries, Leo, Libra or Scorpio owner

Aries   Sometimes you might get so wrapped up in your own life that you forget to include Aquarius. But you love your cat very much. Just make sure you show him how much. He can bring you great joy if you give him attention.

Leo   Don't bother trying to figure out Aquarius. Just enjoy him. If you spend too much time trying to train him, you will be as frustrated as he will. Let him be himself.

Libra   Deep down inside, you admire Aquarius' unconventional ways and wish you could be a little more free-spirited. You two can have a fine relationship if you take the time to play with him.

Scorpio   If you would just watch this cheerful, outrageous cat in action, perhaps you could learn a thing or two. Try to lighten up a little more and watch how much fun you can have with your cat.

TWO PAWS DOWN

Taurus, Cancer, Virgo, Capricorn or Pisces owner

Taurus   You will find it exhausting trying to keep Aquarius in tow. You won't understand why he doesn't play with all the toys you bought him or why he can't sleep through the night. Meanwhile, he will feel like he's in the pound.

Cancer   You need a cat you can hold and love most of the time, while Aquarius needs to feel free. If you try to smother him, he will only become neurotic. There are more compatible cats for you.

Virgo   Only wanting what you think is best for your Aquarius, you will try to mold him to behave and act the way you want. This will lead to frustration. Your cat will win the battle because he won't change. But you will win the war because you will give him away.

Capricorn   You like traditional things in life and that goes for cats as well. As a result, Aquarius doesn't fit the bill. The only way this relationship can work is if you accept him for the weird and wonderful cat that he is — something you're unlikely to do.

Pisces   Looking for lots of love and affection from a feline whenever you want it, you will be gravely disappointed when you realize there are times when Aquarius would rather climb a tree than hop into your lap.

KIDS

Aquarian cats love just about everybody, so this feline will have no trouble adapting to children. Because kids tend to have erratic behavior, they blend right in with Aquarius' mind set.

He and the kids are good for each other because they will play hard. But beware that Aquarius will not tolerate being confined, such as being held too tightly or being shoved into a picnic basket or a cardboard box. He will claw, bite or scratch the culprit no matter how young or old the child is.

FRIENDS AND MATES

Aquarius will find a friend in just about anything that breathes. That goes for humans, dogs, cats, rabbits, chickens, whatever. His cheerful, non-malicious attitude will make any newcomers feel welcome.

Naturally, some signs are more compatible than others. He'd love to team up with another Aquarius. The question is, can you handle two of them? (Can you handle one?) You might try to balance his outrageous personality with a more reserved cat, such as Cancer or Taurus.

As far as Aquarius is concerned, the only signs you might want to stay away from are Capricorn and Aries. They may try to take over the household and force Aquarius to turn into a fighter.

HAIL TO THE CHIEF CAT

President Teddy Roosevelt owned a six-toed cat named Slippers who, like a typical Aquarius, made sure he garnered the proper attention during White House functions.

One night after an important state dinner, Roosevelt, with an ambassador's wife on his arm, led his guests toward the East Room. Suddenly, Slippers dashed in front of the President and then lay down right in his path. Roosevelt, a Scorpio, didn't want to create a scene by shoving the cat out of the way and holding up the procession. So he simply escorted the lady on his arm around Slippers. All the other guests followed, diplomatically side-stepping and admiring the feline — who had found a purrfect way to get noticed.

The Pisces Cat
February 20-March 20

- **Sedentary**
- **Easygoing**
- **Sweet**
- **Docile**
- **Devoted**

erhaps you have passed a house with a fat cat in the window, day after day, and thought it was a statue because it never moved. More likely than not, that cat was a Pisces.

The typical Pisces looks like the Cheshire Cat in Wonderland — eyes half open, with a strange grin on her face that makes you think she knows something you don't know. The truth is, she's not anywhere near as perceptive as the Cheshire Cat. If she thinks about anything at all, it's probably about when she's going to eat her next meal or where she's going to take her next nap.

When your alarm goes off in the morning, don't expect Pisces to get up with you. She will still be in dreamland on your bed because she hasn't had all her beauty sleep yet. Meanwhile, you will be trying to knead that leg cramp you got because of Pisces' habit of sleeping right in the crook behind your knee. Throughout the night, you didn't move for fear of disturbing or hurting her.

When Pisces finally gets up and is finished yawning and stretching, she will wait, without any badgering, for you to feed her. And if she doesn't eat for a while, it's no big deal. In fact, nothing's a big deal to Pisces. That's one of the reasons why almost everyone likes her.

In the world of felines, she's as easygoing as they come. Just let her curl up in a favorite chair or in a warm lap and she's in kitty heaven. If she's an outdoor cat, she will be content to lie on the back porch and let the world go by. She won't stray far because that would be more effort than it's worth. Besides, the last thing she wants is a confrontation with another cat or, worse yet, a dog.

PISCES

Pisces has no interest in proving she's the top cat in the neighborhood. If another feline challenges her, she will ignore him or get up and wander back into the house.

Pisces is a gentle soul. If she has trapped a lizard or some other small animal, she won't intentionally kill it. She will bat it around a bit and then eventually wander off, leaving the terrified creature a chance to escape.

Pisces is not the type to make demands and isn't oriented by routine. So if you're late with dinner, don't fret. Chances are she didn't even notice. And if you are home and got so involved with a long-distance call that you forgot to feed her, she will do nothing more than sit by her food dish and hope you finally get the hint.

There's a certain sweetness about Pisces that makes people want to pick her up and hold her like a baby. And she will love every minute of it. You can tell because she will purr softly and nestle under your chin. For as long as you gently pet her, she will cuddle with you. More often than not, she will fall fast asleep right on your chest and be so relaxed that she will start drooling.

Pisces is one of the most devoted, loyal cats you can hope to find. If you or someone in your family is sick, expect to find Pisces on your bed. Piscean cats have been known to cuddle next to their bedridden owners for days at a time (getting off only to eat and use the litter box) until they got well.

Unfortunately, she's so docile that if a burglar broke into your home, Pisces would open one eye and watch without much interest as he carted off your TV set.

SOCIABILITY

Pisces loves people. If you have company, she will slowly check out everyone and wait for someone to pick her up or pet her. There she will stay, with her eyes at half-mast, until your guest gets tired of stroking her. When that happens, Pisces will move on to the next person in hopes of getting more loving.

PLAYTIME

Pisces is not the friskiest of cats. But she has her fun moments. She will play with her stuffed toys as long as they don't squeak or rattle. She's not into rough-housing, but she will enjoy playing with you as long as it doesn't involve too much energy.

But don't expect to play for a long period of time. Pisces has a short attention span and would rather snuggle up with you than join in any physical games.

IDIOSYNCRASY

Pisces loves to sleep in unconventional positions. For instance, she will lie flat on her back in the middle of the family room with a front paw stretched straight out. Or she will drape herself over the arm of an upholstered chair and fall fast asleep with her back feet on the seat and her head dangling over the side.

HEALTH

Piscean cats are prone to feline respiratory disease. Typical infections produce an unsightly and debilitating condition characterized by sneezing, tearing, inflammation of the eyes and nose, and nasal discharge. If Pisces suffers from this disease, she becomes vulnerable to additional infections.

Pisces Loves ...

- Sucking on strands of your hair
- Kneading the laps of strangers with her paws
- Getting tickled with a feather
- Going along on a hike perched in your backpack

She also tends to gain weight easily, not because she overeats but because she doesn't like to exercise. If you let her, she could turn into the proverbial fat cat.

PISCES

HUMAN COMPANIONS

Pisces makes an excellent pet for the elderly, the home-bound and people with disabilities. She is a companion for life and will always be willing to snuggle.

TWO PAWS UP

Taurus, Cancer or Pisces owner

Taurus   You will get along great with Pisces because you are a home-loving person who will dote on her. Your slight stubborn streak won't bother Pisces — she will just find the path of least resistance.

Cancer   You and Pisces will spend hours together — you with your book by the fire and Pisces curled up alongside you. Your sensitive nature and understanding of this cat's emotional make-up create a warm relationship.

Pisces   As a loving and emotional person, you will enjoy Pisces' sweet disposition. You both could spend the whole day in bed together watching TV. Be careful you don't spoil her. On the other hand, so what if you do?

ONE PAW UP

Aries, Virgo, Libra, Scorpio or Capricorn owner

Aries   You may find Pisces a little too docile. But nevertheless, you can't help but warm up to this gentle feline. She's such a sweetheart that you probably will go out of your way to keep her happy.

Virgo   Your meticulous nature suits Pisces just fine. You will make her life more comfortable than she could hope if you follow your heart. Problems may arise if you make too many demands of her.

Libra   You may want more out of a cat than one that's so easygoing as Pisces. She is who she is, and hopefully you will see that Pisces can bring a lot of love to your household.

Scorpio   You can have a pretty good relationship with Pisces if you don't become too overbearing. A raised voice here and a harsh word there will send even the easygoing Pisces scurrying for cover.

Capricorn   Although you tend to be involved in so many things that you might not give Pisces the attention she deserves, she will understand. Her unquestioned loyalty will make you appreciate her more with each passing day.

TWO PAWS DOWN

Gemini, Leo, Sagittarius or Aquarius owner

Gemini You and Pisces are on different wavelengths. Because she isn't demanding, you won't see her need for attention. Meanwhile, she will feel you don't care — even though you do.

Leo Pisces is just too passive for you because you want a cat with more life and spunk. And the more you try to change her, the more frustrated you and the cat will become.

Sagittarius Your need for excitement and fun may overpower Pisces' quiet ways and unintentionally make her feel very uncomfortable.

Aquarius Always willing to experience new ideas and concepts, you will constantly want to change Pisces' diet or try a different approach to training her. Although you don't mean to, you will just confuse her.

KIDS

As is her nature, Pisces' docile manner will allow children to do just about anything to her, short of pulling her whiskers. But she will not play games that require too much physical activity.

Where she shines is acting as a feline pal for a child and offering him unconditional love. Because she's such a low-maintenance cat, Pisces is easier than most other felines for a youngster to take care of.

FRIENDS AND MATES

Since she's somewhat indifferent to most things, the addition of another pet to the household will not be very traumatic to Pisces. She will remain somewhat aloof for a while until she decides just what this new addition is all about.

If she doesn't like what she sees, she will avoid the newcomer and pretend it doesn't exist. If she does find a new friend, then it's for life — and Pisces will mother and love it completely. Taurus, Cancer or another Pisces will make an excellent mate for Pisces because they are sensitive, attention-loving animals. Their gentle dispositions will make for a quiet household.

RX FOR LOVE

Dr. Albert Schweitzer – the great humanitarian and winner of the Nobel Peace Prize in 1952 – loved a cat named Sizi who acted like a typical Pisces.

Most every day, Sizi would jump up onto Schweitzer's desk, then curl up and go to sleep on the doctor's left arm as he wrote out prescriptions. That posed a problem for Schweitzer because he was left-handed. However, being the Capricorn that he was, the good doctor came up with a solution. Unwilling to disturb the sleeping Sizi, Schweitzer learned to write out his prescriptions right-handed!

Compatibility Chart

I f you know your own
sun sign, *CatAstrology*
can guide you to your
most compatible kitty
companion. Find your sign
along the left-hand side of the
chart on the facing page. Then
read across to see which feline
partners would be:

■ purr-fect (Two Paws Up)

■ paws-ible (One Paw Up)

■ cat-astrophic
(Two Paws Down)

A MATCH MADE IN THE HEAVENS:
WHICH CAT IS BEST FOR YOU?

Owner's Sun Sign	Cat's Sun Sign		
	TWO PAWS UP!	ONE PAW UP.	TWO PAWS Down!
Aries	GEMINI, LEO	VIRGO, LIBRA, SAGITTARIUS, AQUARIUS, PISCES	ARIES, TAURUS, CANCER, SCORPIO, CAPRICORN
Taurus	CANCER, VIRGO, LIBRA, CAPRICORN, PISCES	TAURUS, SAGITTARIUS	ARIES, GEMINI, LEO, SCORPIO, AQUARIUS
Gemini	SAGITTARIUS, AQUARIUS	ARIES, GEMINI, LEO, SCORPIO	TAURUS, CANCER, VIRGO, LIBRA, CAPRICORN, PISCES
Cancer	TAURUS, CANCER, VIRGO, LIBRA, SCORPIO, CAPRICORN, PISCES	ARIES, LEO	GEMINI, SAGITTARIUS, AQUARIUS
Leo	GEMINI, LEO	ARIES, CANCER, LIBRA, SAGITTARIUS, CAPRICORN, AQUARIUS	TAURUS, VIRGO, SCORPIO, PISCES
Virgo	TAURUS, VIRGO, SCORPIO, CAPRICORN	CANCER, LEO, PISCES	ARIES, GEMINI, LIBRA, SAGITTARIUS, AQUARIUS
Libra	GEMINI, LIBRA, SAGITTARIUS	ARIES, TAURUS, CANCER, LEO, SCORPIO, CAPRICORN, AQUARIUS, PISCES	VIRGO
Scorpio	ARIES, CANCER	VIRGO, LIBRA, SCORPIO, SAGITTARIUS, AQUARIUS, PISCES	TAURUS, GEMINI, LEO, CAPRICORN
Sagittarius	LEO, SAGITTARIUS, AQUARIUS	ARIES, GEMINI, SCORPIO	TAURUS, CANCER, VIRGO, LIBRA, CAPRICORN, PISCES
Capricorn	ARIES, TAURUS, CANCER, LEO, VIRGO, SCORPIO	GEMINI, LIBRA, CAPRICORN, PISCES	SAGITTARIUS, AQUARIUS
Aquarius	ARIES, GEMINI, SCORPIO, SAGITTARIUS, AQUARIUS	VIRGO, LIBRA, CAPRICORN	TAURUS, CANCER, LEO, PISCES
Pisces	ARIES, CANCER, PISCES	TAURUS, LEO, VIRGO, LIBRA, CAPRICORN	GEMINI, SCORPIO, SAGITTARIUS, AQUARIUS